Vicki:
You are one in a [...]
Enjoy. Affectionately,

2006

blooming
twig books

WWW.BLOOMINGTWIGBOOKS.COM

ANITA'S HEAVEN

By NORMAN OBER

Inspired by Letters Channeled From Heaven
By Anita Ober

June 1993-August 2006

NEW YORK

ANITA'S HEAVEN
Norman Ober
www.anitasheaven.com

Published by
Blooming Twig Books
East Setauket, NY

ISBN 1-933918-11-x
ISBN(13) 978-1-933918-11-2

The author is responsible for the contents, possible errors of printing, spelling or grammar, fact or omission, and holds all parties blameless for the content and/or distribution of this book.

"There are more things in heaven and earth, Horatio,
Than are dreamt of in your philosophy."
Hamlet, Act I, Scene 5

In Memoriam
Anita Ober, 1919-1990

We dedicate this book to our Daughters
Dody and Amy and their families

Leslie
Richard
Timothy
Laryssa
Michael
Conner
Kailyn
And
Bailey

FOREWORD

Isa and Yolanda Lindwall, Founders of the Lindwall Foundation, have shared their remarkable Releasing Program for mending minds and bodies in 40 countries during their 34-year chiropractic practice. Their ever-expanding relationship with a 'Supreme Source' radiates through their work and lives, towards the goals of unconditional love and healing. Visit them online at www.lindwallreleasing.org

For those who have felt separated from loved ones following the transition called 'death' and still seek words of reassurance from the 'other side' about what happens to a soul after leaving its physical body, *Anita's Heaven* can provide comfort and peace of mind.

For those who research, or are interested in the use of Kinesiology, we hereby go on record to affirm that our personal tests indicate that Anita's letters contain an unusually high percentage of accuracy. We encourage the reader to keep an open mind while reading this book, then make his/her own evaluation.

To our dear friends, Anita and Norman, we thank you for your deep love and dedication in manifesting this pioneer documentation.

Dr. E. E. Isa and Yolanda Lindwall
('Doc' and 'Ruth' Lindwall in the manuscript)

ACKNOWLEDGMENTS

We give grateful thanks to all those named in this book, alive and departed who informed, taught and inspired us. Among our living benefactors are Doc and Ruth Lindwall of Planet Earth and the spiritual cosmos; Myron McClellan, a wise, empathetic and far-seeing mystic in Denver, Colorado; Jean Houston whose incredibly foresighted words and books opened us to a new universe of spiritual awareness; Tom Cowan who initiated us to the mysteries of Shamanism; our niece, Doris A. Ober of Dogtown, California, a multi-talented writer and author's collaborator, for encouragement and guidance her old uncle needed, Kent Gustavson at Blooming Twig Books, who showed us how to finish and format a book we'd been brooding over for 13 years, and to Nicole Holmquist at Blooming Twig Books who found the heart of this book and threw a spotlight on it for others to see. Thanks, too, to Benita Ober for superhuman understanding and support through trying periods of writers' preoccupation and isolation; and not least Brianne Kelly-Bly for tireless first aid to Norman and his loved-hated computer.

Among many others whose remarkable writing narrowed the gaps between knowledge and ignorance are Deepak Chopra, Sogyal Rinpoche, Leon Uris, Raymond Moody, Helen Greaves, Martin Luther King, Baird T. Spalding, Dan Brown, Michael Baigent, Richard Leigh, Henry Lincoln, Tim Wallace-Murphy, Sanaya Roman, Marilyn Hopkins, Christopher Knight, Robert Lomax, Simon Cox, Duane Packer, Howard Murphet and Arthur Dobrin. Credit is also due to countless hours prowling the Internet and discovering medieval to modern differences of opinion on religious dogmas.

AUTHOR'S NOTE

"Anita's Heaven," distilled from over 3000 channeled letters, began three years after Anita died and continues to this day. I was as unfamiliar with telepathic messages from the afterlife as you may be until, after three years of relentless search for my lost love, our channeling began. Its great effects on me are part of the fabric of this book.

We hope others who have lost loved ones will find in these pages a positive way to deal with their grief, to open their hearts to love again and above all to love God.

Anita's letters shed strong light on God's miraculous, wondrous and unshakably humane paradise – the stories of new arrivals, heaven's topography, its universes, its tasks, its humor, its limitations and His long term aspirations for humanity.

Our book may disquiet rigid orthodoxy by doubting that God could conceivably have given *any* one group the only keys to His Kingdom. Anglicans to Zoroastrians, they've all proclaimed themselves to be the guardians of His wishes and rewards.

Anita's letters destroyed my atheism and taught *me* love of God without dogmas or interpreters; though she herself favors organized religion with strong lay oversight.

Whose God is real? Is He the menacing one cited by theorists who maintain their power by their interpretations of Him? Or is He today an all-loving spirit who created and affectionately seeks only the best for us? This book may help you decide which God is real for you.

Finally, as you'll discover, words Anita channeled to me evoked memories, large and small, of touching, humorous and unforgettable events we shared during our years together. These, flashbacks in *italics* throughout the book, illuminate our personal story and love for each other that has never died.

Norman Ober, August 15, 2006

ANITA'S HEAVEN

by Norman Ober

"Until I'm with thee, thou abidest in me."

INTRODUCTION

Most of what you are about to read stemmed directly from channeled letters I've received from Anita in heaven since 1993. I "wrote" this letter to her in love and gratitude thirteen years later:

Darling Anita,

I still call you Neetery, which was your brother's name for you, or Nita, which your mother called you, or Neets — I never knew where that came from. By any name, you changed me from a retard at loving anyone but myself to a decent husband, father and friend. You gentled my overeager passion and put me in touch with my potential to share, to give and receive love.

"Not content with improving me in life, you rescued me from the hell of despair and gave me reason to live without you by finding the way for us to channel. You pried me loose from atheism and from my certainty that there was no future after life; you drew me a roadmap back to you.

"There's no way to thank you except just to adore you for the life we had together and the magical afterlife that's ahead. I thank God for you and you for God and for the fact that I can thank God, knowing you're with Him. I love you.

Now we can get on with the Introduction, starting with a distant memory of one day on King Street, Dorchester, Massachusetts: Freddie Hannon, a seven year old neighborhood friend - my age, too - said to me, "You don't believe in Jesus? You're going straight to hell!" Freddie jumped back in fright to avoid being swept across the Styx with me.

To his surprise nothing happened. My brilliant riposte was, "You're nuts."

That incident with my neighbor in Dorchester, Massachusetts, helped shape my views of the Boston Irish. And for most of my adult life, I 'bah-humbugged' anybody suggesting Freddie's Christ or my family's God created us or our planet. I was an atheist.

At the outset, let me assure you that I have no special power. I'm not mystic, psychic, a medium or any sort of swami with paranormal gifts.

My beloved and painfully missed late wife Anita believed in our God Jehovah all her life. It took more than a year of her channeled letters to turn me around, until which time I must say I was the last man in the peopled worlds to help write and edit this book.

As a boy, I chanted halting Hebrew without understanding the words until an English translation of the Yom Kippur (Day of Atonement) service told me I was begging forgiveness for a long list of uncommitted sins. That made me shun my family's religion until our Daughter Dody told Anita she wanted a bat mitzvah (confirmation).

2

World War I was ending when I was born in Boston in 1919. I was the last (my siblings insisted the least) of five children of Michael and Augusta Ober. On the only voyage of his life, my father proved to be an adventurous little boy. On the way to America with his parents, Joseph and Celia and his older Sister Rose, he was lost for several frantic hours until they found him sleeping soundly in the engine room.

The Obers-to-become hailed from Kisvarda (by some accounts Kleinvardein), Austria-Hungary. Later it was Hungary and later again Austria, I have read, as wars moved the area's borders back and forth. A third child, Ethel, died there in infancy.

The family got the name Ober from a Civil Service customs clerk with a bad ear. Nobody is sure now, but it might have been Haber, Hoffer or Auber. What's undisputed is that Joseph and Celia begot the rest of their eleven children in East Boston.

Michael left school from the fourth grade and worked all his life to help keep his parents' big family afloat – then his own. After twenty-one years working with Irish laborers, he spoke their brogue naturally all his life.

He operated a freight elevator for the American Can Company where he met Gussie, a comely, strong-minded fugitive from czarist pogroms. Her first and only American job was hand-soldering cans. They met when he, running a freight elevator that immigrant workers weren't allowed to ride, tried to explain to her that she had to use the stairs. She didn't speak a word of English. She rode up. It was love at first fight.

He, handsome, short, stocky and strong as an ox, planted himself on the street above her subway stop in East Boston Sundays, turning back rivals for Gussie's hand until she was his. He had to get help from someone called "the old man Cohen" who assured her worried parents that Mike wasn't Irish but as Jewish as they were.

I was born at 48 Hansboro Street, Dorchester, in a back bedroom where my mother's welcoming screams were less audible to passers-by. At four, I was already eye-to-fist with anti-Semitic Irish boys, girls and parents encouraged by Irish clergy, teachers and police. Years hating Irish Catholic anti-Semites left a mark on me, as you'll see.

I Graduated from Boston Public Latin School, class of '36. Two weeks later I interviewed for a job as a bus boy at the old Thompson's Spa in Boston's diminutive newspaper row. Everything was fine until my interviewer read on my job application that I was Jewish. She told me summarily I wasn't eligible for the job. When I asked why, she said, "We've found that Jews aren't happy working here." Interview over!

I moved to Manhattan two years later to share an upper West Side apartment with my Brother Emil and to find a drama school with a good scholarship program. Instead, I grew a mustache and got a job with a marionette company at 18, saying I was 24.

I was an avowed agnostic at first, sure that people who hated and hurt had no God telling them to do it. I remember my words to a pretty Catholic girl in the cast of a Barrie play we were rehearsing in Boston. It was in 1937 after I graduated from high school. She'd just come from confession. I told her it was like confiding her secrets to spies.

After five years of puppeteering from the East Coast to the Mississippi, I had a tenuous toehold in radio acting and somewhat more success writing radio dramas. Then I met Anita Rosenblum, who believed in God but not me when, on our first date, I said I was going to marry her. When she saw I was serious, she let me keep my promise.

We were married in 1943 when I completed U. S. Navy basic training. After a four-day Gotham honeymoon, we drove our bought and borrowed furniture to a cottage at Sampson Naval Training Station in upstate New York.

Six months scripting "Sampson Goes to Church," "Mission Accomplished," "Blue- jacket Time" and other up-the-Navy broadcasts didn't qualify me to write about Anita's afterlife, but when her letters started coming from heaven they began my basic training to deliver the essence of what she channels me to this day.

Sometime between 3:30 and 6:00 a.m. on April 24, 1990, the tenth day of the forty-seventh year of our marriage, Anita Ober left everyone and everything she loved, quietly surrendering herself to cancer while I was asleep next to her.

Six weeks before, her illness was diagnosed as primary hepatoma. Internists, radiologists, doctors of complementary medicine, an oncologist and my brilliant cousin Bill Ober, a noted pathologist who loved Anita, agreed - nothing could save her. Anita accepted it with dark stoicism and tried to prepare me to live without her. I stampeded her through examinations and alternative measures until a week before she died.

At home without her, desolate, for months I descended on family and friends and drove or flew to Elder Hostels in cities Anita and I had visited. Anita's absence followed me every mile. The months I waited for my grief to ease only showed me that I couldn't adjust to losing her and would never forget her. From God I expected nothing.

My parents believed in Him. The two youngest of five siblings, my Brother Harold and I listened to our oldest Brother Ralph extol socialism and atheism, both echoed by our next older brother and sister, Emil and Doris. Both of us eventually decided they were probably right and, hedging my bet, I announced that I was an agnostic.

When Doris died at 21 of influenza-pneumonia and Harold at 25 of Hodgkins Disease, I decided that, if there was a God, I hated Him. My father falling to Cushing's Disease at 71 and Emil succumbing at 47 after two pioneer heart operations honed my vendetta. For years, in acerbic arguments with friends and foes alike, I labeled the un-reasoning faith of the Boston Irish as blind stupidity until I thought it was out of my system. After thirteen years of channeling, I learned that it was still in me.

When Anita died I berated Him just in case He was out there. "Damn you. You took her, send her back!" "A real God wouldn't let Anita die - and while we're talking, why doesn't time heal my wounds?" Or I just yelled, "Take me to her - now!" His silence proved I'd been right all along - I was dealing with a bogus God or none at all.

Even while I climbed the walls trying to will her back to me, I couldn't believe Anita was gone forever. I expected nothing from my efforts to reach out to her until our letters began and gradually convinced me Anita is in heaven and of Who's in charge there. What follows describes my efforts to contact Anita, how our channeling began, how I was unsure about our letters until Anita's persistence broke through my doubts.

PART ONE

Like their mother, my daughters Dody and Amy believe in the survival of the human spirit. Worrying over my unabated grief, they urged rethinking atheism and putting a brake on my bullheaded diplomacy if I wanted access to Anita. It was a hard sell for someone who took no stock in the tooth fairy, Santa Claus, leprechauns *or* God.

My antipathy for the Boston Irish began simmering in 1924 when our family moved from a Jewish to a mostly Irish neighborhood in Dorchester. Eligible to start kindergarten, on the first day of school I walked down Train Street towards the Harris School with some friendly children until a little girl asked me what church I attended.

I explained that we went to synagogue. She was puzzled. I said we were Jewish. Without a word, a wiry slim boy bloodied my nose. "You killed Jesus!" he said. It was the first blow but far from the last. The time came when my Brother Ralph set up a boxing ring in our basement and taught me how to fight.

Later in the book, I say I never met a Roman Catholic I didn't like. This is the place for my one exception. The toughest kid in our neighborhood in Dorchester was a slightly older boy named Al Franzoza. I was afraid of him. Every kid I knew was.

Early Christmas Eve (I was probably thirteen) my folks had company. Their friends the Kaitzes drove over from Chelsea. Their daughter Jeannie Ruth, about six, was the prettiest child you can imagine with her doll-like voice and eyes and her ringlets. I couldn't take my eyes off her. We were playing on the street near the house before dinner with a few other kids. Along came Al Franzoza. I hoped he wouldn't stop but he did.

He was taken with Jeannie Ruth and like a boy training hard to be a crude man, came up with a crass vulgarity aimed at her. "You better get out of here," I quaked. The next thing I knew, I was on the ground, paralyzed with fear, sure that I was broken somewhere and mortified that I looked bad in front of my little guest.

I jumped to my feet and hit him back. He began dancing like a boxer, jabbing, pummeling me, left and right crossing. I knew the end was near but I couldn't back down in front of Jeannie. So I fought back. Remembering my Brother Ralph's advice to carry the fight to my opponent, I held my ground.

We slugged it out, it seemed, for hours. People went by. One said, "Peace on earth, good will towards men," in sardonic acknowledgement that it was Christmas Eve. But nobody stopped the fight. A few stayed to watch. One instructed Al to flatten the Kike. I landed some solid punches but I knew I was losing. I was wrong. I found my legs and he lost his. Suddenly, Al burst into sobs, turned and fled. I had won the fight with the toughest kid in the neighborhood. What was left of my face was saved and my reputation made. Except for a few non-fatal drubbings, I won most of my fights after that.

About five years later, I thought prejudice, racial slurs and bruises ended with our move to Wellington Hill in our old neighborhood. By the time I left Boston for New York in 1937, I saw myself as an actor, budding writer and friend to the world. But a surprising second opinion from heaven, which you'll read near the end of this book, shook me up by telling me I still needed to exorcise hatred burned into me in Dorchester.

By the time our Amy and Richard Flanders were married, I saw myself as a slightly short tempered liberal. At the wedding rehearsal Anita and I met their good friends, Doc and Ruth Lindwall, spiritual healers and ordained ministers. They travel the world repairing lives, getting their marching orders from Spirit Most High.

That day, Anita said she sensed an aura about the Lindwalls. I didn't, but quickly saw what a unique, loving, admirable couple they are, even if I did suspect them (then) of practicing voodoo.

The Lindwalls were due in Manhattan in August 1991 for a weekend "releasing" workshop. My unabated campaign to recapture Anita was going nowhere, so, with urging from my daughters, I put my skepticism on hold and enrolled in the workshop.

Under Doc and Ruth's supervision, Amy said, the collective energy created by participants' cumulative emotional currents could bring remarkable results. When the Lindwalls conducted earlier New York workshops, Anita and I attended pre-weekend releasing demonstrations twice, but I balked at going to the whole workshop both times.

How or whether Doc accessed buried memories of past lives baffled me, but we had seen him free a young woman from chronic despair by uncovering her memories of her last death and that of her young son during the Holocaust.

Not sure it wasn't macabre vaudeville, I tacitly doubted that the Lindwalls could draw Anita back to me. Their Saturday session began with en-

12

rollees pairing. Doc said the right pairs instinctively team up, guided by Spirit. (Sure!)

Once partnered, we spread our blankets on the floor, put our pillows and tissue boxes down and got to work. One on each team facilitated, coached by the Lindwalls and their staff, while the other spoke, sometimes laughed, cried, and occasionally became hysterical. Doc, Ruth, and their assistants quickly restored calm when anyone in the room was overwrought. After lunch, partners swapped roles and the work continued.

I thought I facilitated well Saturday morning. Reflecting, I realized the credit was due to my partner's practiced inventory of grievances and tears. In the afternoon, I aired my needs and waited for something to happen. It didn't.

On Sunday I partnered with a bright young college professor suffering from frequent depressions. She resisted my efforts to draw her out. Finally, I called an assistant over, who identified her problem – my voice was like her father's. He being a key player in her pain, my words were a wall between us. We did better after that.

Following lunch, I stretched out on my blanket with my tissue box at hand and my partner soon prodded me to explain how I hoped to reach Anita when I didn't believe in God. Sometime during the exercise I became aware of an odd throbbing in my abdomen.

I ignored it but it persisted. Suddenly it struck me that this might be some sort of sign. That brought me to my haunches, blurting, "Anita, is that you?" I tried telling my partner what was going on. She settled me back on my blanket with no interest in my quirky symptom, but the pulsing continued. Afire with hope, I reached for my tissues and cried from my soul, "Anita!" The pulsing continued until, suddenly, it stopped. Driving back to New Jersey Sunday night, I told myself it would come again and it did.

In bed about a week later the throbbing started again. I cried aloud, "Anita?"

A single beat charged through my viscera. "Are you doing it?" It was repeated.

"Can we communicate this way?" Again a pulse!

"Does a beat mean yes?" Pulse! "Do two beats mean no?" No reply!

Asking whatever I could think of brought me bundles of beats or none. Then they stopped. My heart sank, but the beats were back a week later. After more floundering, I thought to ask if no beat meant no. An explosion of pulses tore away the curtain.

For several months we communicated this way. Our "dialogues" consisted of my spoken questions and Anita's pulsed yes or no, with nothing yet written down. I have sketchy memories of affirmations that Anita loved me, was happy, rid of her cancer and had reunited with departed family members and friends. She adored every minute of her blissful afterlife in a fabulous place where nobody was ever unhappy.

Pulsing frustrated me. Anita could answer yes to questions like, "Are your mother and father (Abe and Lily) there with you?" but couldn't reply when I asked, "What do you do with yourself? What do you look like?" Worse, contact was erratic. I tried every night, but first a week, then longer, went by with no

15

result and I was sure I'd lost her forever or that pulsing was the invention of my bereaved brain.

I told my daughters I thought my mind was going. Amy assured me with a straight face that I was crazier before the pulsing. As to my fear that I was making up her answers without Anita's help, Dody and Amy insisted that, if I kept at it, I'd figure it out.

Amy had a disturbing theory. It seemed to her that pulsing might be enervating for Anita in her ethereal state, requiring her to recover energy between episodes.

That I was draining her was a knife in my heart. Would I lose her? Were our exchanges delusions? The next time we pulsed, she confirmed that the effort did sap her and that our connection was weakening. But she urged me to ask more questions.

Our sessions continued sporadically a few months more, with the gaps growing until pulsing stopped altogether. By that time, expecting it to happen, I saw the process not as my antidote for grief but as a way Anita truly found to respond to it.

I can't pin down when our pulsing hiatus began but I know when it ended. Visiting Dody's family in Colorado in Spring1992, I explained to her how our contact started at the Lindwalls' workshop and ended at my home in White Meadow Lake.

Dody suggested that we look for literature on pulsing and drove me to a splendid Denver bookstore, "The Tattered Cover," that has a large section on spiritual phenomena. For two hours we found nothing about pulsing, but we did find books on automatic writing, described below, which I later identified as channeling. One book titled, "A Testimony of Light," by Helen Greaves, gave what struck me as a credible account of the author's unexpected communication with a departed friend.

Ms. Greaves recounted how, evenings when she customarily wrote, she felt the presence of her late dear friend, Mary Frances, who had been an Anglican nun. One astonishing night, the author suddenly saw that *she* wasn't controlling her pen.

Mary Frances had begun the first of *her* letters from heaven! If that account was authentic, I thought, Anita might be able to guide my hand in spite of my bad attitude about a place whose existence I doubted.

I proposed automatic writing to Anita verbally and, with great discomfort, asked God to help. I sat every night with a pad and pen ready, waiting. I

17

tried to empty my mind but that effort invariably stimulated swarms of vagrant thoughts, mislaid memories, surefire story plots, what-ifs, conversations, obligations and irritations. In my worst moments I was sure mean spirits were barring me from their world, if any.

I resorted to badgering God again. What did I want that was so terrible? Anita didn't ask to die. I didn't want her to. The phrase, "until death do us part," was just a line an antiquated hack writer thought rolled nicely off the tongue.

My bellyaching ended at 7:15 a.m. on June 23, 1993, three years and two months after Anita's death, when her first written message trickled to my pad:

"This is Anita. I love you. I'm happy. I'm well. I'm still your wife. If you want to join me, I'll be here when you arrive. I'm learning many things I can't wait to share with you. I'm signing off but we can do this again, dear Wob. Love, Tata"

Tata, a nickname acquired at Sampson Naval Training Station when we were WWII newlyweds, was as near as our next door neighbors' toddler Patsy Herbert came to saying Anita. We were enchanted with the child and I began calling Anita Tata, too. The nickname Wob was short for Wobbly. Anita called me that awhile. It was after we saw the movie, "Bambi," one night at Sampson (Thumper's description of how the baby deer looked the first time she wobbled to her feet).

Our first letter troubled me. If Anita really channeled it, there should have been something revealing about heaven. I concluded that I concocted it.

18

Aloud, I begged Anita to convince me I wasn't writing to myself, that this *was* automatic writing.

The same night she answered. "Darling, you wrote what I impressed on you. We can write this way. I love you and miss you. We had a wonderful marriage, darling."

There was more. Anita confirmed that my cousin Bill Ober, who had just died, was with the Ober family, still skeptical. "But he's brilliant; he'll find his way here." In closing she said for the first of many times, "Stop scribbling and go to sleep. "It's late for you. Time is very different here." My penned scrawl says it was 11:45 p.m.

I wasn't sure I hadn't composed the second letter, too, but Anita's reference to "impressing" words on me was something I wanted to hear more about.

Note to Reader: I should explain that I began by dating each letter, but you'll now see the dates stop. The reason is that when I started assembling her widespread references to the same subject into solid blocks of copy, dates running back and forth confused me and I think would have confused you.

In our earliest channeling, we talked about everything and nothing, ecstatic that we found each other. Anita's letters were a delicious blend of love, information, happy memories and projections for our future when my time here ends. I wallowed in every word and hungrily asked for specific details about heaven; how they communicated there, what they did, did they reincarnate and if so, how? It took me a while to rein myself in - Anita was still learning and could tell only what she knew.

But there was enough information from the beginning to hold me enthralled. June 24, 1993, the second day of our correspondence (we did two the first day) brought our third communication. "I'm 25ish now. My light body (defined later) stays that way. Yours will, too, when you're here. We live in the present tense - time doesn't pass as it does in life." I pestered her often about heaven's timelessness; it was hard to believe.

Anita switched subjects. "When you start one of these letters, our vibrations come together. Sometimes I'm asleep and you wake me, but sleep isn't as much fun as this is."

"Heaven's on no map. The route from life to afterlife isn't linear. It's dimensional. My soul can go to you by detaching (to be defined), or to Waymart, Pennsylvania, then Amy's home, New York City, her brother's, or Colorado, Dody's."

We met on New York's West Side in 1941. Anita was a kindergarten teacher at Columbia Grammar School. She had excelled in every course at Ethical Culture Normal School except mathematics and got her teaching certificate by promising her math professor she'd never teach arithmetic. (Or **learn** it - she refused to write checks or balance our checkbook. I told her, "You **have** to know how. Something may happen to me!") During her last week she said with sardonic satisfaction, "Learning about checks would have been wasted. Nothing happened to you – just me."

Visiting her classroom, I found Anita on hands and knees making believe she was the engine of a choo-choo train, steering her squealing, scrambling mini-students under and around the furniture. She augmented her low pay by babysitting some of her little children at 50 cents an hour. When parents complained that their prodigies were bored at home except when she was there, she told them, "Stop drowning them in FAO Schwartz (now defunct) stuffed toys. Let them play with bottle caps and lids. Give them clean rags, pots, pans and little potatoes they can get their hands around."

She followed her own advice. Dody was born early and never stopped to rest. I came home from my writing job at WCBS Radio one night to the sight of our besmeared darling in her Baby-Tenda, joyfully kneading a slice of raw calf's liver with both hands. Telltale evidence stained her pudgy pink arms, shoulders and face. Anita, preparing dinner, dismissed my sputtered objections. "Look how happy she is!"

My first lesson in Anita's outlook on life came after our first date, when I said at her front door that I intended to marry her. She responded by fleeing inside. I wasn't impetuous. In love with my golden girl at first sight, I restrained myself an infinite week.

21

Another of Anita's letters answered a question of mine. "We're encouraged to get a full night's sleep and when awake, not to waste energy that makes everything work here. It's never implied that there may be a shortage, but nobody squanders it."

Celestial sleep habits: "It wouldn't be heaven if we had insomniacs. We don't. When I lie down to sleep, it comes immediately and lasts as long as I need it to. If I lie down, perchance to daydream, sleep waits. When I'm done I sleep."

I asked Anita if she dreamed during sleep as in life. She answered, "We don't dream at all. Influences that trigger dreams don't arise until after reincarnation. There are no pressures. Being *awake* in heaven is a perpetual dream."

In forty-seven years together we nearly never went to sleep angry. Usually, Anita drifted off in the middle of a sentence, her words suddenly segueing into soft breathing. Later, when I managed conventions for the Council of Jewish Federations and our girls were grown, Anita, working with me, wanted me to control my temper over last minute changes demanded by participants, management and staff. I tried being Mr. Nice Guy my first year, but same day requests, ignored by hotel staffs, disrupted multiple meeting turnovers and shattered our timetable, as milling crowds scrambled to get into and out of meeting rooms. Often, still angry at me over my outbursts at the saboteurs, Anita kissed me goodnight coldly, saying, "This is only to let you sleep. If you don't get some rest, you'll be worse tomorrow." God, I miss her caring – and waking to quick swishes of mouthwash and her velvet lips!

She channeled, "Consciousness of being here, as it does after all past lives, leaves us when we're born again. What scatterbrains we'd be if memory of past incarnations and celestial interludes stamped themselves on our conscious minds. Nobody can retain the impressions and activities of dozens of life spans and still handle new identities and the important details of each present life."

Here's an important detail - on May 12ᵗʰ, 1943, my twenty-fourth birthday, I decreed that there would be a six-week reign of terror every year, during which I should be given compleat conjugal fealty and obeisance until her birthday came even with mine. Her big brown eyes tried to appear to be frightened, but she quickly pummeled, hugged and kissed me. My annual effort was a failure, but we were happy.

Anita was a visibly <u>unhappy</u> girl when we met. Later she told me her hasty, short-lived first marriage had just been annulled. One look into her sad eyes told me I had found my future as she sat stitching a seam down the backside of pantaloons tacked on the winged puppet Icarus. I'd rewritten an earlier version of a puppet show about the history of flight for a High School English teacher named Grace Stahl but said I had no time to direct it. As soon as I heard Anita volunteered to help out, I found the time.

Anita said fairly early in our years of channeling that everyone goes to heaven. "This is no-fault paradise. Nobody is punished or excluded. God trains us here to live in peace, harmony and love and we do. On His planets, he wants domestic, national and international disputes settled civilly, regardless of who has the power. Can you take the absence of anger here? You Taureans are harder to separate from your tempers than us naturally sweeter types."

*She **was** naturally sweeter, with all five feet, two inches of her loving children, me, animals and especially cats, defining newts, deer, garden snakes and more or less every creature*

23

on foot or belly as pets. After WWII she took on reforming me and counteracting Dody's spirited enthusiasm for her daddy's assorted songs, stories and comic gaucheries. Anita's public person percolated down from her Latvian mother's diffidence. Privately, she shared a gentler variety of her father's Romanian ardor as she patiently nudged me to civilize mine. Trying to be as good a mother as she was a teacher, Anita did her best to deflect Dody's precocious challenges, then to help Amy outgrow her efforts, as a child, to be as invisible as Ensign Pulver of "Mister Roberts."

Anita channeled. "We're all good here, no matter what we did in life." Later she makes it clear that includes souls from nine presently peopled planets.

"The saying, 'Man proposes but God disposes,' isn't true. I see a God of love who has eternal hope for His creations. Too often, power disposes and God must mourn. If He had total control, life on the planets would be what it is in heaven."

"God's advisors sometimes wonder if there isn't a better way. Why is there no hell here? It's because hell, Dear Norman, lies not in our afterlife, but in our selves.

"You have to be here to believe how peachy pleasant everyone is. It's the perfect place to love thy neighbor. Carping and criticism are out. Kind words spring from every lip. Anger's checked at the Pearly Gates. Think you can hack it?"

I asked, "Pearly Gates?"

"I didn't come through any," she wrote. "There's no St. Peter here – nobody is called a saint – passage to heaven is on a no-questions-asked basis. The good and bad get the same reception. If they don't tell, we don't know what they did where they came from. Very few say things like, 'I'm an axe murderer. I don't belong in heaven.'"

Anita's sense of humor waned only during frequent critical self-examinations. No feature of her face or body escaped her disapproval. From her silken ash blonde hair ("It's mousy!") down to the soles of her feet ("They're flat!") she saw flaws. I argued, "All your bad features add up to beautiful!" Her skin was slightly olive. Every chance she had she browned it in the sun. Her small ears dissatisfied her. "You can't find them." Her straight, unblemished nose (like her mother's and Dody's), she claimed lacked character; she said of her delicate facial features, "I'm anonymous." She called her teeth dingy, her smile crooked. Of her fetching feminine proportions: "All I can wear in public is an A-line cut dress. I'm too short to be so wide" - breasts "too big," buttocks "a shelf (Both lies!)." But the warmth of her smile and her genuine love for people lit her from within. She "did" her own hair and nails, sewed and knitted her own clothes as a Navy wife and loved bagging bargains at S. Klein's on Union Square, the May Company (14th Street) and Orbach's (34th Street) during enthusiastic forays from Stuyvesant Town.

In one letter Anita disputed my claim to having the patience of a saint: "They're Earth inventions. Planets subscribe to every species of deity and special messengers. Their mythologies are derivative, too - religions on most of them, like on Earth, pitch for new believers by swiping and slanting each other's divinations."

"When God created people, they didn't form solid ranks of theists in His Image. All planets still have fewer practicing believers than part-time pretenders and covert or open unbelievers. Many arrive here with *no* concept of God or heaven. Without knowledge of the afterlife they need lots of indoctrination."

Anita thought about the end of *her* life. "Death was easy. A warm glow lit my passage, wrapped itself around me like a baby's blanket."

The stretcher that bore her body down the stairs from our bedroom was covered with black plastic, strapped tightly. The undertakers had difficulty getting it around and down from the turn to the stairs from our narrow bedroom hall. I watched anesthetized as they eased it to the living room and left. I was impatient for the others to leave - the police and medical examiner who responded to a reported home death. I remember wanting to go back upstairs and tell Anita about my bad dream and to see if she needed anything. When the last were gone, I did go upstairs to our bedroom. She wasn't there, or the bed sheets they wrapped her in. I sat on the mattress and cried. I'd made a terrible mistake letting them take her. I whispered to her, "It won't happen again."

"When my soul came here," Anita channeled, "Mother was waiting. Daddy came soon after. I was still their little girl. I was so relieved - cancer couldn't kill me again."

"Death is so beautiful. Leaving my body, seeing no others at first but sensing warmth, I passed along a lighted way. I wasn't walking but impelled. I wasn't sure where I was going until I was here. I knew something was alive in me – and where could I be going but where others had gone before me? I mention that because, when it's your time, I want it to be as lighthearted, undoubted and warming as it was for me."

Was this the girl who danced the Lindy, the Peabody, and the Miserlou, a wistful old Grecian folk dance that took off big in 1962? Was this the Anita who adored Noel Coward's plays and songs and loved "A Chorus Line" so much that, at seventy, the year she died, she still gamely accompanied the original cast album, doing her one-woman version of the entire company singing and dancing "One (singular sensation)?" Dody saw her do it during a visit and declared, "Stop! You'll die!"

Was I the brash, ambitious boy who left Boston at eighteen for a stage career, acted in marionette shows and radio dramas before some primal signal ordered me to erase the sorrow in Anita's eyes? The walls of my computer room are a gallery of photos. Every day over the desk three twenty-four inch pictures of Anita, framed side by side, look down at me - on the left, at thirteen, sizing me up with definite reservations; center, Anita's wedding picture, radiant, smiling lovingly; and on the right, at sixty-nine, still wreathed in natural beauty, showing her pleasure during the theme dinner of a Marriott Masters meeting planners weekend in Palm Springs a year before she died.

Also hanging there: Anita's baby picture, cap-and-gown graduation portrait, snapshots with her children, with pets, as a sun browned counselor at a children's summer camp, a group

27

photo of her sorority Pi Epsilon, a group photo of our wedding dinner at Billy Rose's Diamond Horseshoe and assorted shots of our daughters, Dody's Timothy and Michael, ourselves. (Newest 2005 additions: Anita's Great Grandson, Conner Reece and her twin Great Granddaughters Kailyn Anita and Bailey Corrinne).

My first channeled letters were written on paper pads, with Anita urging me to ask questions. I could barely write *her* words legibly and omitted mine until some time after we discovered that I could print them out on the computer. On September 10, 1995, two years and three months after we began, Anita began explaining channeling:

"Both of us being completely receptive is the key to automatic writing. My instructor said I'd reach you if you're open to it. You sure were. With my instructor's help – he's a Taurean, too, with a pious look and the light body of a cranky ballet dancer - after an earful of your cursing and moaning, he changed my mantra to 'Nooorman' and helped me adjust my frequency until it locked on yours.

"Remember what Doc Lindwall said about meditating? 'Just concentrate on Anita and you're meditating.' I concentrated on you – on your image. I don't send a beam. I sat quietly and thought of you until I wobbled onto you. It can take longer than it did, but you bombarded me with such energy that it was quick and painless.

"Once our frequencies locked, we were one again telepathically, minds aligned. There's no magic box, no antenna, no gadget. It's done with love and the strong mutual desire to reach out to each other.

Anita wrote, "As Shakespeare put it, 'There are more things in heaven and earth, Horatio, than are dreamt of in our philosophy.' I had no confidence when I started my first letter. With nothing prepared, I blurted and you scribbled. It wasn't much – I wasn't sure I was getting anywhere. But you got it and I was overjoyed!"

To make automatic writing (channeling) clear, I'm consolidating here most of Anita's information on the subject, something I'll do with other key subjects that appear sporadically in her letters. Her very first brief reference to channeling was on 6/24/93: "It takes concentration but doesn't drain me as signals to your abdomen did."

I must have asked later if others channeled this way, because she wrote, "Some contact is vocal. We may learn to use our voices or another person's." (I campaigned for vocal contact but it never happened.)

9/29/93: "Lately you concentrate better – there's less mind wandering. But your meditation's so-so. Practice being in a thought-free cocoon longer and longer." (God knows I tried, but I've never really gotten hold of meditation as others have.)

On 10/12/93 Anita reported, "I had another channeling class. Some people at your end, born good at it, come to heaven as naturals, but we have to work at it. Now I use my mantra and breathing exercises to help me start. Try a mantra."

"Distance doesn't affect channeling. If it did, your time and space junk would defeat us. You call in my vibrations and they get into your head.

"Neither of us being psychic, we can't talk verbally. When you speak, I hear you, but you're not ready to receive me that way." That led her to write that she didn't "hear" my voice but my thoughts. "We won't *hear* each other speak again until you're here."

Anita's voice was soothing, modulated, clear, below alto but not masculine. Her gentle tones echo in my mind. Sometimes I called her my Marjorie Mourning Dove because her Upper West Side Manhattanese (dorg instead of good Bawston dawg, etc.) tickled me. When she was angry, her speech level escalated half an octave. She claimed marriage was her license to civilize me and consistently tried to tone down my incisive sarcasm when affronted by ill-informed attacks on my unassailable logic. "Keep it up," she predicted, "and we won't have a friend left." She was wrong. Over 300, many dead now, came to Dover, New Jersey to pay their respects at her memorial service.

11/27/93: I tried channeling through my computer to see if her letters printed. It worked. Not only that, but the keyboard made possible much longer letters for us to luxuriate in, have fun with and to tease and bait each other. More important, I began getting Anita's steady information stream on paper that stays readable unlike ink on pad paper that blurs as the paper deteriorates. I was never too tired to channel.

In WWII I was a seagoing weatherman and hand-typed the ship's newspaper on stencils aboard the APA 69. While I was at sea missing her Anita worked for a men's

31

haberdasher in San Pedro and slept in a rented room with a Murphy bed. Later, cousins of mine

moved her in with them in Hollywoodland and she wrote that she took a sales position in the

children's clothing department of The May Company, Los Angeles.

We exchanged two to three letters a day. Hers came in batches when the USS Carlisle

hit port and my stack of censored letters left the ship. I typed mine. She penned four to eight pages

at a time that gave me sanity-saving love transfusions.

The Bosun's Mate tipped me off that officers in the ward room were reading my letters

aloud to each other and suggested I tone down the personal stuff. I responded by writing more

often and soon he said my letters went unread until port was in sight.

She wrote one about swarthy Mexican laborers whose lower halves she had to length-

sized for jeans. Others were filled with home news, chatty hopes, plans and prayers for peace to

reunite us. I responded with tales of liberty at unnamable ports, when the crew staggered back to

the Carlisle at or above alcoholic overload - and with my never-ending pass-the-censor details of

my life at sea.

(Author's note: Unless there's a compelling reason, this is where I stop dating the letters. The more I disrupt chronological order by consolidating individual subjects from all over the book, the more later dates that follow earlier ones muddle the mind.)

In another letter from heaven Anita channeled: "When you send your thoughts, I 'hear' them as if you were speaking aloud. If I'm busy, I catch up with them later."

"If we didn't love each other, you could have taken any path you wanted away from me. But your poem at my memorial service said it all. 'From the pain of our parting I ask no relief.' If I *didn't* love you I'd have responded to that."

Anita

Inscription weighs in memory more than word,
Empowered more when written than by tongue.
Endearments forgotten soon after heard,
In ink endure, most precious thoughts among.

A year of retirement, sublime and serene,
Blest a middle class knight and his queen.
Too late the warning date, January Sixteen;
Death took eighty-nine days to intervene.

I awoke, you near but still, by fate's lief
Your sweet soul stolen - beyond belief!
Though I no longer hold you I cling to my grief.
From the pain of our parting I ask no relief.

Brown and soft with warmth Anita's eyes;
Her limbs and cheeks reflect the summer sun.
Silken, golden hair in beauty lies
Atop a vision only sightless shun.

Gone the staff your precious being lent,
Your radiant heart forever spent.
Mind, wit and wisdom shared in privacy
And our unmeasured, treasured intimacy.

Your low-toned laughter so like a song
Resonates within me though you're gone.
So soon our separation is overlong,
Our days and nights apart wrong, wrong, wrong.

Back to our letters: I must have asked Anita if channeling drained her energy as pulsing did. Her answer was, "It leaves me exhilarated. I'm never sad –

except a pinch when you are. I love every letter. If we end one and start another, it won't tire me."

I asked Anita how much she gets out of Broadway shows I attend. Her answer was, "I visualize them through your mind. What you see transmits to your brain. I pick it off there. It's not exactly seeing or hearing, but the effect is the same. My problem with shows you go to is, if you look away I miss what you do. If you hate a play, it's hard to get past your mindset and form my own opinion. It's fine as long as you like what you're watching. I never hate plays you like."

We loved going to Broadway shows, especially musicals. She enjoyed dressing up for theatre with her mink coat and hat whose short tails she called minkies. She insisted I dress, too. "To sit in the dark?" I demurred. "No, to be with me," she purred. "Lady in the Dark," "My Fair Lady," "Lady, Be Good," "As the Girls Go," "Bloomer Girl" "Carousel," "Oklahoma" and other big musicals that glorified the soft species satisfied Anita's love of memorable music and lyrics and mine for my sacred feminine.

"Since our letters started," she wrote, "I've been sure more couples would channel if both believe in God and think it's possible. Living atheists don't try to communicate with departed loved ones. They think nobody exists after death.

"The hardest thing for you to accept yet is that words I imprint on your mind aren't your own thoughts. Logically, with no voice contact, where but into your mind *can* my letters go? I can't get them written on your computer except by impressing them on your brain - not your feet or belly button.

34

"How many times have you said, 'I just got an idea,' or, 'What made me think of that'? When it happens, can you be sure I didn't put it into your head? Which reminds me, projection or impatience – *whenever you butt in creatively* I steer you back on track."

Anita called me to task a number of times for anticipating her thoughts. "If you want to start letters, do it - but as you, not me. When you type in my words ahead of me, I don't know if you're backsliding or can't resist editing what I haven't said.

"Don't jump start me. Let me do it myself. Write as *you* and let me come in as me. You're fine awhile. Then I sense you writing my next words. Re-member, I imprint, you write." (I did my best not to but now and then the devil made me do it.)

Now and then Anita answered a question that was in my mind. "Do I know your thoughts when we channel? My knowing what you just didn't say answers the question. We're tuned in always, though at times I do have to leave you on your own.

"I don't usually tag along when you're out walking. Sometimes, when you're in the car, my awareness mutes. I'm not in touch all the time, but as Myron McClellan (the mystic mentioned earlier and introduced later) told you, I always get your message."

More: "Your state of mind comes through when we do this. I can agree or disagree, but access to your mind helps me respond to your moods.

I *thought* I understood that and changed the subject. "Do you breathe oxygen and nitrogen and exhale carbon dioxide as we do?"

Her answer was, "Only our borrowed brains 'breathe.' Expelled air is as clean as what's absorbed."

"When I'm preoccupied, I spy on you in short takes. When I'm really preoccupied, I 'read' your messages later. I listen lightly when I talk to others, still keeping connected to you. That happens scores of times every day."

"I try to sleep when you do. It's not simple. I know when you think of me. When we think of each other, we connect. Yes, I can read your mind."

Anita read my mind when she was alive. I never lied to her; I'd never have pulled it off. I was constant to her for forty-seven years, sure that her radar or mine would blip if I strayed. In truth, I never met a woman worth destroying her happiness and our marriage over and nearly never regretted it. She knew when I was tempted. I complained to her about it after taking wide detours around infrequent opportunities.

The next night Anita had a whole new subject for me. "An aborted, fully formed fetus, like anyone departed, gives heaven soul seeds to retrieve. We don't receive a fetus any more than we do a corpse. Only the mind and soul come here.

"Discarded bodies become dust. My soul left my body before cremation. My death didn't sadden me; it relieved me. Even my sorrow for you diminished in heaven's hands. Death is God's instrument for retrieving our souls after life ends. Escape to heaven should be celebrated."

Later I asked, "Do you read my mind when we're not channeling?"

She said, "I peek in. Between letters I maintain muted awareness of you but usually tune out your mind. If I didn't, I couldn't concentrate on what I do here (described later).

I told her to help herself to anything she can find in my mind. We knew we were attached spiritually if not physically. "If we were meant to break off when you died, we wouldn't be channeling. You tell me to skip writing often. Do *you* want me to?"

"I don't want you trying your new wife's patience." (By then I was married again. Anita had urged it - details later). "I just feel we shouldn't let too much of our good thing intrude on Benita's (sic) happiness."

"You say you want a role in the work of the Light. Our letters could inspire others to value honor and love, too. If our experience helps other lovers contact each other after one dies, what a glorious dimension it would add to our love."

To make sure of it, I asked Anita, "Is what we're doing telepathy?"

"That's exactly what channeling is. Let's try exchanging thoughts on our channel right now. I'll think something to you. If you sense what I thought, we'll have another way to communicate."

I told her to think away.

After a pause, "I said, 'I love you.'"

I hadn't heard it. But it was worth a try.

We talked about departed relatives often. In July 1993, when he checked into heaven, Anita had a reunion with my fabulous cousin, Doctor Bill Ober. He was a year younger than I, a product of Brookline, Mass., Harvard University and the Boston University Medical School, courtesy of the U.S. Army - also of his own elegant self-portrait. He became a distinguished albeit eccentric pathologist, medical writer and author of extraordinary articles and books, among the latter: "Boswell's Clap," a medical and social analysis of venereal diseases of various literary figures, and "Bottoms Up," a scholar's tongue-in-cheek study of sexual peccadilloes of past cultural personalities.

My Father Michael and Bill's Father Harry were two of the eleven born to my Hungarian immigrant grandparents. My brothers, sister and I thought our Ober grandparents were cold, stern, and scary. I had recounted to Anita their nasty habit of kissing their grand-children on the lips. And very weird, their whole apartment house on Bremen Street, East Boston, reeked of Sulpha Naphthol, a powerful disinfectant.

I knew Billy Ober when we were kids. Someone once said we looked alike. I saw it, but Bill, at eleven, was visibly outraged at the idea. We didn't become friends until 1948, after he reeled into our lives at the door of our Stuyvesant Town apartment, tipsy and uninvited, declaiming, "I want to meet whom or what my cousin married!"

Anita instantly adored Bill Ober. She force-fed him black coffee, doted on his idio-syncrasies and forgave his social sins and addictive smoking. Like his father, Bill was an iconoclast. In his accents: "If I cahn't have my sherry and cigarettes, life's without purpose and I'll have no paht of it!" He died painlessly of a ruptured aneurysm, delighted it wasn't cancer, stroke or a heart attack as his doctors had predicted.

"Bill's doing fine," Anita wrote. "Being here has sobered him somewhat. His Father Harry, though, doesn't change."

My Uncle Harry was a difficult, disdainful personality all his life, worshiping his self-image, scornful of anybody not himself. He had taken his well-crafted persona to heaven and become a familiar, if not notorious oddity. Anita described how he set himself up in a public park and inveighed to passers-by against "the fraud that there's a God." He attracts good humor, indifference or silence - not ridicule – there's none here - and a small following that enjoys his challenges to God to come out and debate him."

"Harry urges Bill to stick with atheism," Anita wrote. "Bill is keeping him at bay. Harry's like a stubborn child. Rebecca (Harry's wife) believes in God. Bill's grandparents do, but Rebecca's loyal to Harry and his supporters apparently feel as he does - a tiny minority clinging to disbelief. I don't know how anyone experiencing this miraculous afterlife can question Who makes it work - but that's your Uncle Harry."

Next morning, Anita continued, "I was just warming up when you fell asleep on me last night. I was talking about family - I must mention them as often as I do God.

"The deeply convinced of all religions, arriving here, experience great inner joy in the confirmation of their belief in Him. The rest of us range from once lukewarm believers to atheists in life. My father (Abe Rosenblum) has a private name for overly devoted new converts in heaven, 'eyeball holy hallelujahs.'"

Anita's parents and mine were doing well. She wrote that she had a message for me from my mother: "She says she loves you and is proud of you for writing again, that she loves *me*, and no longer gets 'the bean.' She says to tell you, correctly, she is beautiful now and Mike, your Father, is handsome."

The bean was my mother's expression to explain after the fact her major outbursts at life's roadblocks. Mother Gussie's family, safe in Boston from Russian pogroms, forever after called America "The Gan Eden" (The Garden of Eden). I remember a fight promoter discovering my oldest brother. Ralph, who, in his teens, fought like a tiger. The promoter accompanied the underage boy home and asked Gussie to sign a contract for him to manage Ralph as a fighter. She raised her broom. He fled. My mother ruled us, a tough little tsarina with intrusive expectations no daughter-in-law ever lived up to.

Anita updated me on my Sister Doris and Brother Harold, who had died, as noted earlier, and my older Brother Emil, gone since 1961: (They were later joined by Ralph, in his middle nineties, who, as she told me, lost little time reincarnating.)

"Doris and I are good friends. She busies herself in the arts and lives with an artsy crowd. You'd be proud of Emil now. You remember his womanizing.

40

He's very different here, serious, studies and lives practically a monastic life. Like Bill Ober, Emil was surprised to discover himself toeing the mark here.

"Your Brother Harold's darling. He's been happy since I arrived. We talk, hug and yes, kiss - as brother and sister, in case you're wondering - and you are."

During Anita's first visit to my family in Boston, which was near the end of Harold's battle with Hodgkin's disease, the two discovered that they looked strikingly alike. Harold said, "Put a mustache on her!" It was mutual love at first sight. When our visit ended, Harold put a piece of paper into Anita's hand. On it in pencil was:

> *If Norman should ever displease you, that lowdown miserable crook,*
> *There's always a fellow named Harold, that wonderful, cute little schnook.*

Anita mentioned her Parents Abe and Lily often. The three of them share frequent meals, visit one another and attend lectures, entertainment and public events together. Mealtimes are, she writes, as gemütlich as they usually were in their second floor apartment, across from his dental office at West 72nd Street and Columbus Avenue.

Lily lit the stove or oven as soon as she saw the lights go out in his office. He enjoyed dinner at home except when he was in the doghouse and they ate in silence. Things were different when their son Robbie was home from school and/or when I dropped in - Lily made it clear even before Anita decided she loved me that I was welcome. Anita's Brother Robbie maintained that, when I was there, the food was better.

This is what Anita wrote me much later (January 16th, 2005) when I asked her to describe mealtimes with her parents in heaven:

41

"Food is fuel here, health matters more. My father doesn't have arthritis pain from leaning over patients or painful arthritic knots in his fingers. Mother's ecstatic over having her voice and mobility back." Lily's stroke left her speechless and paralyzed.

"Here, my parents are young lovebirds who speak nothing but adoring words. Daddy's billing and cooing aren't much different from the way he carried on alive. Lily will surprise you. She finds no fault with him! The words darling, little Russian and Froo-froo-frau, still on his lips, don't embarrass her.

"They come and go together, share books, have outings, some with me, visit around, travel, see shows, whoosh off on tours at will. Daddy paints and she watches. He knows he's no master but enjoys doing landscapes here - and seascapes from memory.

"There's always something to talk about. If I'm there I tell them about you, my Receiving clients or about group work. They're always interested in you, second only to Robbie. They have their eyes on him now and we pray he (her illustrious brother, Prof. Robert Rosenblum) recovers fully from cancer surgery. (He did). We'd love him here but don't root for him to cross over. He has too much to live for.

Anita occasionally helps her mother do volunteer work with the youngest arrivals - something Lily did at the Children's Hospital in Manhattan for many years before her stroke. Most of Anita's comments on heaven's babies are lined up consecutively now:

"I love to be with Mother and her little charges, prematurely here for so many reasons. Some newborns die of genetic flaws. Some were perfect but unwanted. Many were victims of brutality, lust, want and disease. It's ludicrous but children miss parents who abused them. We give them so much love that, when they recover, they're anxious to return to life again. We don't have Medicare, we have tender loving care."

Anita observed, "Compared to my job in Receiving, it's more relaxing working with Mother's babies and children. All they really need is love."

"When there are no known family or friends, as with orphans, stillborns, the aborted or babies abandoned at birth, volunteer angels look after them. *Anyone* suddenly deceased takes more effort to sort out than anticipated arrivals. If family doesn't come forward, angels do."

"In my definition of a perfect world, people capable of loving and fostering happy, secure babies would get them and people unable to provide happiness and security wouldn't. Heaven gets too many wasted children."

Do stillborn babies have souls? Her answer was yes. I doubted it until Anita wrote, "They thrive with loved ones surrounding them! Stillborn babies find generations of antecedents here. Like aborted fetuses, they come to full term, eventually receive light bodies and become fully developed adults at about twenty-five.

"Usually there are ancestors eager to care for and love them. The planets' unwanted babies and children are better off here than abandoned in plastic bags or orphanages, foster or adoptive homes. Even favorably adopted children are never entirely whole without real parents or real angels to rear them.

"Parents and/or earlier generations provide the love that gives children senses of self in a playground of endless joy. No place is safe as heaven's embrace."

Anita first heard that births not engineered in heaven, usually involving unmarried and underprivileged mothers, didn't qualify for heaven. When she learned better, she wrote, "Even in pregnancies outside of His coital alchemy, once on the way, babies become part of God's cycle of life."

"God rotates us all into and out of life. For better or worse, babies born without 'credentials' receive God's love. Consider the numbers of stillborn, abandoned, aborted and murdered babies. They're a huge population here."

"In Receiving, mothers who died in childbirth always ask if their baby is alive. If it isn't, its mother brightens right up when she learns she can raise her child here."

44

Later Anita dropped it on me that, before birth, some fetuses *get cold feet about being born!* "Still in the womb, some intuitively decide against coming to term. A stillbirth is often a soul that *changed its mind in the womb*.

"Seem far-fetched, does it? Mind grows in the womb. Who can argue that a fetus gets no intuitive reading on its future? Drawing on encapsulated memory, some elect to return to the magnificence of heaven and try again to find more promising parents.

Who thought of such possibilities in my much too sparsely ill-spent youth in Boston? In those feverish years, my few successes were dogged by fear of the p-word! One such liaison - I wasn't yet seventeen - produced a near miss by way of a late period. It makes me shudder to think I might have married young and never met Anita. After that uncollected wage of sin, I never completely trusted contraceptive measures.

Anita continued, "That babies may decide against birth should give right-to-lifers pause. Millions are born on the inhabited planets. Is it unthinkable that, along with the many uneventful and sometimes premature births, some in the womb, instinctively distrustful of their prospective environments, self-abort?"

"Birth produces from genius to bubble head. Bottom of the barrel babies are explained by blaming your wife's family. But injuries, physical flaws or chemical failures may cause mutation, idiocy, physical defects, *or* fetal suicide."

I went to bed brooding about fetuses aborting themselves. The next night she was waiting for me. "Doubting again, Thomas? (*See John 20:24-29*)

45

Calm down. A fetus doesn't consciously control its destiny.' Reason begins at birth, but fear begins in the womb.

"This is especially true in pregnancies when both prospective parents and the developing baby have reservations. If the expectant parents oppose abortion, the fetus may decide for the three of them. In-body fear of abysmal prospects may move it to back off and try again. We're also taught that delayed or prolonged births come from last minute changes of heart. Here the word is that babies do form impressions in the womb."

Then Anita turned both guns on anti-abortionists: "Right-to-lifers don't believe *all* people are free and equal. Over drinks they reveal rats' nests of anti-feminine prejudice and fanatic drive to hold absolute power over female bodies. If they were really concerned for the fetus, they'd use the money they put into propaganda, guns, lobbying and blockading into medical care for pregnant girls and find homes for babies they say deserve to live. And, by the way, we believe *a fetus is not a living baby until it's born.*"

"Anti-abortionists terrorize women who try to end their pregnancies. They attack freedom of thought and women's rights to choose. The religious right, Muslims, Iranians, Iraqis, Neo-Nazis, the entire population of women-dominating cultures (few had heard of the Taliban by this letter) want to nibble away women's choice, deliver them to ultra conservatives and undo sexual equality where it exists.

"Rightists hate sexual equality. A woman's place is under her man, mouth shut, legs spread! They say they're saving babies but their target is feminine independence. I can't speak for God, but women's rights are as woeful worldwide as in Sarajevo, Rwanda and other parts of Africa. As for the souls of stillborn and aborted fetuses, they're re-cycled, not murdered. They're *saved*, not destroyed."

In June 1919 in upper Manhattan, Anita Rosenblum was born after three days of labor, black and blue, misshapen and frightening to behold. Her father took one look, rounded up his three brothers, and The Four Roses went to the nearest bar to get drunk. In several weeks a beautiful baby began to emerge from the battered infant who recovered from her birth ordeal to begin her journey to me.

Finally, on babies, Anita said flatly, "Aborted fetuses *are not regarded in heaven as having been alive*." I wondered how that would sit with right-to-lifers who claim private lines to God's mind.

Anita mentioned angels earlier. There was more: "You just read about angels in TIME (Magazine). There really are angels, whose relationships with God are grown into. With God's direct influence over human behavior limited, angels here are His primary workers on the planets. When their missions imperil them, other angels rescue them.

"Pure of heart or sinner, after we cross the line from life to death, we all eventually become angels. First I thought there were none. No winged entities flit about here. But we all serve Him, even though we don't flap wings and pluck harps.

Anita and her mother had an uneasy truce of tolerance when I met them. Lily had perfected stony silence as a way to discipline her husband and children. By her twenties, Lily's unexpressed but implied disapproval of Anita's growing independence as a woman inevitably changed their relationship for the worse. Anita's impetuous first marriage, which lasted nine months, was an ill-conceived effort to break her mother's passive chokehold. (Anita's first groom, of blessed memory, made me look good).

The birth of Dody and then Amy gave Anita and her mother loving common ground and restored their mutual affection. In 1977 after Lily's stroke, no daughter could have done more to care for her through eight years of speechless purgatory.

Our children remember Lily before her stroke. From birth Dody adored her; Abe, too. Amy doesn't remember Abe's year of lavish affection, when he called her his little mustard plaster. Her Nana's non-verbal love suited our quiet child. When Amy attended Barnard College, she moved into Lily's West Side Manhattan apartment to help care for her. Speechless and paralyzed, Lily Rosenblum died of pneumonia in her own bed.

Sometime later, Amy became inexplicably uneasy in the apartment at night and took to sleeping in her old bedroom at our West 79th Street apartment. When Doc and Ruth Lindwall returned to Manhattan for another releasing workshop, Amy invited them to spend three nights at her apartment. Over dinner she told Doc about her uneasiness.

When they retired Amy slept well. In the morning Doc said her grandmother was still in the apartment, afraid to move on, and that he had reassured her she'd be safe crossing over. He was ready to help if Amy agreed. She hesitated but did.

Doc said no more about it until the next morning, when he announced, "Grandmother's where she needed to go. She was afraid she'd fall into a void." The apartment never discomforted Amy again.

When Amy told me about it, I queried Anita. "Mother said what made her hold back was, not believing in God and realizing she still existed as something, afraid of the unknown, she clung to the apartment."

PART TWO

Anita, through our channeled letters, campaigned vigorously for me to believe in God. "You acknowledge Him now because you rationalize that I can't be here alone. Accept God first, then that I'm here with Him."

"God just is. But He's not the God of pulpits where He's defined for the benefit of clergies. God doesn't any longer require, judge, demand, condemn or criticize - but bathes all human life equally in His loving kindness."

I used to discourage Anita's lighting Sabbath candles and going to synagogue. She lit candles and prayed over them Friday nights anyway, and went to synagogue on high holy days, suggesting I go along, too. I went grudgingly when I did, asking always, "Why should I atone when I have nothing to atone for?" I found something.

After a year or so of letters cynicism lost ground and my atheism beat a retreat. A reluctant crawl in that direction provided the time I needed for it to anneal and to accept our channeling as real. Still, she was dissatisfied. "I'm not comfortable with love you pour on me when you show less for God. For me, help Him reveal Himself to you."

As her letters continued, I caved in but Anita wanted more. "You accept Him but don't see yourself part of Him. Nobody has to worship here. Some do anyway because love of God is natural to us. We're at peace contemplating Him. Religions make loving God obligatory, but He loves you and asks nothing in return. Love Him back."

She channeled further, "We look for ways to help here 'for His name's sake,' to be good to one another because His example inspires us. He proscribes nearly nothing and has no religious rules. We simply want to live up to His hopes for us and so we do."

Anita gradually made me comfortable believing; after five years of descriptions of her world, I considered myself completely cured of atheism. But she kept at me. "Saying you believe was a giant step. Sometimes, though, you still suspect the smallest bit that the left side of your brain writes these letters to the right side or vice versa. You've always said nobody changes anybody's mind. I've done as well as one spirit can, nudging you from atheism to what - uncertainty?"

I was uncertain the day Anita and I met Doc and Ruth Lindwall at Amy's wedding rehearsal. He sized me up clinically, identified my diabetes by kinesiology, consulted his Spirit Most High and advised me that I had been a rabbi in an earlier life, had become disillusioned and was slain for speaking out. Then he showed me how to release my hatred of those responsible and forgive myself for hating. Anita, more impressed than I, beamed when Doc prescribed releasing regularly to quell my quick temper and we were both to learn how perfectly Ruth Lindwall partnered with Doc in their perceptive healing.

Our letter ended, "I keep nudging you because believing people are happier people! Time doubting is time out of happiness. Am I beating a dead horse?"

I said, "Flogging an old geezer, but I feel the love, not the lash. Keep it coming."

53

Anita fed me many facts about heaven as she proselytized: "Scads of us come to God when cancer or other disasters kill us. You'll appreciate how His simple diet restores youth and maintains health and vigor. Then there's youthening.

"Youthening physically doesn't regress our minds. Older people who come here get younger bodies but remain mentally mature." Youthening was Anita's word for elder arrivals' physical transformation to what she always calls the mid-twenties. Later she explains how heaven ages souls who arrive before their middle twenties.

"I never wanted to leave you, but paradise provides life without lies, cheating, robbing, killing, wars or any form of hatred. Notably terrible persons get special attention before being free to gad about." I learned something about this in the Helen Greaves book, "A Testimony of Light." Helen's Anglican nun tells her there's an established process for private counseling of wicked people before they're ready to roam about heaven.

Anita described heaven's menu as, "…basically liquefiable and consumed by our energy systems like cars use up gasoline." Before we weigh in seriously on food in paradise, let's first look at the arrival process through letters about Anita's impressions of her first job there, in Receiving. Then we'll do the same with her collected observations on young light bodies fitted to new arrivals, part of indoctrination to the afterlife.

When she was ready, Anita told me about her job in Receiving and how people become and stay young. "Souls arrive intact without bodies. They're treated briefly when necessary. What we see and hear telepathically is a compact soul visible to the eye. Usually family is alert to the passing. If there's nobody to tell us the language he or she understands, we play a sentence in different languages until we get a soul response.

"We talk mind to mind. Automatic translation *really* kicks in when the soul is in its light body, which happens fast in most cases. We tell newcomers they're in heaven, that the past died with the body, that a light body will be provided, restoring audible speech and hearing, also that a home will be ready with or near family or friends.

"When I can't answer a question, I find someone who can. Sometimes I'll say, 'I want to make you comfortable with God's love and for you to think about the kind of life you may want to have here. I can schedule you for interviews about your choices.'"

Anita reflected, "If they're curious about God, I may say that one-to-one prayer is permitted but not required. Heaven is where we all go anyway when we die. In Receiving we do orientations, not inquisitions, but we sometimes encounter petrified souls who need more reassurance than we can give and we schedule help."

56

Then this: "Receiving is now getting a flood of souls from Rwanda, Africa. Rwandan outrages touch us all, but don't stir anger. Inductions to heaven are something like yours into the Navy. You sent your civilian clothes home. Flesh, bones and attitudes left behind, we don new bodies and acquire new attitudes."

I could have sent my civilian clothes to Boston. Anita and I weren't married until after my Navy basic training, but she was by then the magnetic center of my world. Not sure I'd live to see her again, I sent her my civvies to hold for my return.

Anita said she learned these things in Receiving: first, that she was changed but still had life; second, that atonement for mistakes wasn't necessary in heaven; third, that afterlife is everyone's reward for the struggles of living; and fourth, that God isn't vengeful but sees humans as victims of flawed efforts to create loving humanities.

"I speculate as you do on why residents leave heaven voluntarily. But departures more or less cancel out arrivals. Can you imagine what it would be like if nobody ever left here for a new life?" Trying to picture paradise packed to its rafters with every generation from the beginning of time, I saw Anita's point.

On the same subject: "Ancient and modern catastrophes have required new housing areas to open here quickly to accommodate sudden surges of souls. But housing areas pack away as easily as they spring up."

"The number coming from and returning to the ten planets (later, she discovered the number of peopled planets had shrunk to nine) is simply staggering. You can't guess how many of us it takes to process victims of mass murders, saturation bombings and natural disasters. Cataclysms keep us busiest settling victims in."

When TWA 800 crashed, I asked Anita how that large group of passengers was handled. She wrote, "Sudden catastrophes are always surprises. We call in extra help. If the soul is intact we get identities and notify Records that they're here. They post family names by radio bulletins. Someone sees or hears the name, tells family and they come.

"While we interview, other staff works on housing. With family input, homes get extra rooms or new homes are set up nearby. Arrivals are connected to food service. Fitters issue light bodies and clothes. Then there may be more interviews.

"Souls may come traumatized. Even if you accept right off that you're in heaven, you need to get comfortable with it, especially if you were an atheist or a criminal."

The next evening I asked Anita if Flight 800 victims knew what happened to them. She said, "I briefed a group of adults' and children's souls from that plane. None knew what happened. There was an explosion. Some *thought* it was a bomb; but cause was followed too quickly by effect. It may never be certain what sent the plane down. Reconstruction and examination by your experts will be more reliable than our guesses."

Anita wrote again about her own trip to heaven, "I came straight through a warm, bright vault of light. Mother was waiting. She said it was to make sure I didn't linger as she had. Other souls coming at the same time had their greeters.

"I hardly noticed I was moving until I became aware of – I want to say ascent, but it wasn't up, down or sideways – my soul *advanced* to Receiving. Before a word was spoken, telepathically, of course, Mother being there told me heaven was real and you were wrong about that. Before we reached Receiving Lily answered my first questions."

Even though Anita mentioned it several times, I couldn't picture what she talked to before it had a light body. She'd said the soul arrives naked and communication is telepathic, but I asked, "What's visible?"

"A tiny version of what God looks like when He's among us. These essences 'think' as they spoke in life. Some believe they're still alive. I've been 'thought' things like, 'Am I going to make it?' I tell them they already have. I say, 'You're in heaven' and promise they're going to love it as I do.

"Many want to go back. We tell them about reincarnation. They usually want to return to living loved ones until they understand they can return only chemically, as newborns. When that's digested they usually settle down and ask about their options."

"Options" calls to mind a solemn rite of our marriage. When Anita came up with some especially sweet word or deed – at the dinner table, making light of my temper until we were

alone, being the doting, cooing mother she was to our babies – whatever – I'd say, "That did it! I'm picking up your option for another six months." When I repeated it over the years, her pleasure over my beneficence became conspicuously less evident.

She said, "I have fun with atheists in Receiving. They can be led from arrival through getting their light bodies without believing they aren't hallucinating.

"George somebody was sure he was in a prison hospital. When he died of AIDS, he *knew* there was no afterlife. He decided he wasn't dead. A man like that can be stubborn. I explained again but he kept telling me to quit kidding, where is he *really*? Finally it seeped through that he's in heaven and that how he lived won't hurt him.

"The more convinced he got, the nicer he got. The nicer he got, the more tiresome. If I didn't have to deal with oddballs so often, they'd be funnier. I remember this George saying, when he figured things out, 'Let me get this straight. You're not an angel, just another dead person sitting here. What's in this for you?'"

We sat in comfortable chairs at the crematorium and reminisced about Anita – Bill and Rhoda Ober, Amy and Richard, Dody and a few close friends. My chair faced a brick wall with a closed metal door. Through a glass window, a low blue and yellow flame was visible at the bottom of a horizontal vault. The flame would be turned to high when we left. Thirty or forty minutes passed in restrained recollections. Finally, a discreet attendant said it was time to go. We filed out slowly. For years, I lost her there again and again.

Anita had another Receiving story on a later night, not a happy one, except for the woman's arrival in heaven. "Anna came from her deathbed after fifty years of marriage. She bore her husband seven children, was a good Christian, mother and wife.

"Her husband never really talked to her, *never*. Instead – they were Indiana farmers – he clunked in after each day on the land and expected sex. During her menstrual periods they had sex. If she was ill or tired they had sex. She never enjoyed the act, which he preferred before he cleaned up for dinner.

"He never took a day off or gave her one, except when she went to the hospital for each child. She was never ill – she felt he wouldn't put up with it. She loved her children – he saw them as expensive investments working off their board. After their seventh, her body stopped producing offspring.

"They never celebrated a birthday or anniversary. There was only farming, animals, sex and meals. One by one, the children moved out. Then he talked, complained about their disloyalty. Her load grew heavier as she took on more farm work.

"One morning he came down and she didn't. She didn't know what took her, but had thought for years death would be her only escape.

"I began my routine. She thanked me politely and said she always felt death would be better than life." Anita concluded with, "I'm going to try to keep up with her."

"People arrive from all planets. Some fall on what we tell them. Others, as you heard, don't believe us right away. Young people ask what there is to do for fun. We describe the recreation but, if they ask, tell them there's nowhere to buy cigarettes and hard liquor or beer; no pool rooms, no street gangs, no social dance halls.

"Some youngsters say it's a drag and want to go back at their ages at death. Usually there's a girlfriend, wife, boyfriend or husband they want to rejoin. Their reactions to learning there's only one road back are touching."

"We try to have a light body fitted right away. That's routine. If a soul is damaged or uncommunicative, we get expert help." A case in point is Arnold Lipkin, Anita's cousin. who was blown up piloting an Air Force plane during WWII. The remarkable story of his restoration is coming up shortly.

"Now that I know heaven, I look at prolonged suffering before inevitable death as barbarism. When you do the book, be sure this gets in. It's appalling keeping incurable patients alive because of misguided morality that ignores the pain of the dying."

"Felons and killers are tame and pliant here; maybe it's because they think they deserve to be punished. If they do worry, they don't for long."

Anita on housing: "Everything necessary does itself. You don't see construction workers putting up new homes. Whoever does it probably spills subdivisions out of jars."

62

Following the Swissair plane crash off Nova Scotia, Anita wrote about *its* victims at Receiving. "There's no nice way to describe an in-flight explosion. Passengers don't all die immediately; some survive until the impact of a crash."

Anita and I flew often in our last joint career, booking and planning meetings. She was timid about flying, nervous until we were airborne. After a few sips of a double scotch or bourbon she relaxed. "If anything happens now I'll die happy."

"Sudden death interrupting life," she wrote, "takes a second or less. The soul usually arrives intact. But even a soul fragment is enough to rebuild a body. People can be forgotten quickly on the planets, but God so loves us that destroyed souls are restored. It surprises newcomers to realize they're 'talking' without bodies. There's no predicting who'll remember how they died and who won't.

"Empathetic families are easily found for loners, illegitimates, outcasts and people who don't know their antecedents. Locating kin after sudden death takes longer. When it's a family member, known or not, relatives are especially eager to help."

Another observation: "The devout aren't surprised by heaven, but they are to discover they're here on equal terms with former human scum they knew of in life. Picture yourself learning that every fiend, rapist and killer imported from the planets has a haven in heaven. It shocks believers to know that being religious puts them no closer to God than unbelievers. We count on families to help them come to terms with that."

"Allan Gentry arrived during your night, a victim of AIDS after a nasty downhill course. His name isn't Gentry. I promised not to use his real one. He doesn't want his family mentioned and I won't.

"Allan asked if he could be openly gay here. I said he could be whatever he wanted, but not physically; that heaven welcomes same sex friends and lovers, but that homosexual love, like all love here, borders on platonic.

"Allan said that his lover, still alive, gave him the disease without getting sick himself. His lover cheated with other men. As his AIDS grew worse, his partner was increasingly distant.

"Our job in Receiving is to listen and counsel. Allan said talking to me was already heaven. For the last three years of his life, nobody listened to him. Clinic and hospital staffs were professionally polite, but few met his need not to be shut out as he shut down.

"Other gays tried to help but the number of AIDS patients overwhelmed them. Nobody knows what to say to them when they're dying."

Anita on the light body: "It's not a gaseous sack. It has substance that you, a cuddler who loves touching, will approve of. We try to have light bodies and clothes issued right away, just off the Receiving area."

I asked for a description of a light body and Anita obliged. "They're temporary shelters for our souls until reincarnation, when a real body starts to grow again. You can't see through a light body. It's not hard, like a doll's; it feels almost like flesh."

Anita promised me, when I said my arrival in heaven would most likely result from diabetes and heart problems, "You'll get an instant overhaul here, and be remodeled to twenty-something (as close as she came in a place that didn't measure time). In life you're flesh, bones, valves, tubes and fluids. By maturity, they're in trouble. Light bodies aren't vulnerable frames for weakening parts with hazards of slow or sudden death lurking from head to foot. Light bodies are efficient soul outerwear. Early versions had imperfections. Now they're just right. Light bodies outlast their occupants. When you vacate yours it goes to a new soul coming to heaven."

Over the next five years she added more facts: "Light bodies are neither hot nor cold but temperature neutral. We never perspire or feel chilled. If yours doesn't work just right, you get it fixed or exchange it. If you develop vibrations, drag-leg or any abnormality, you whoosh to a body shop – that's what *we* call them – for diagnosis and repair while we wait. I haven't had to, but Daddy did. Something affected his stability. Normally it's not busy, but around then a lot of us had the same malfunction."

"We don't exactly breathe," she told me in another letter. "It's unnecessary. On the planets, oxygen is essential for survival. Here only our brains need oxygen. A light body brain ventilates independently of nostrils, through pores in our scalps. The tiny openings aren't visible. If I put a hand on mine I feel no intake or output. Our air is pure. We don't need protection from airborne pollution or dust.

"Eyes help us avoid bumps when we whoosh ourselves about, but personal radar is what really keeps us apart as we pass one another. Our ears automatically hear or tune out sound; no voice is too soft to be heard, none too intrusive to be tuned down. We're relaxed and carefree. Nobody cries. We have no tear ducts. There's no hay fever and nobody coughs or sneezes. All heaven is 'air-conditioned' and germ-free.

"Neither sex has fingernails or toenails - not needed. Nobody attacks. Light bodies face no threats to the joy of being, so they have no unnecessary armor. Our souls, hearts and brains never have to fight or run away.

"We're human forms for cosmetic reasons, I suspect, and because brain functions require walking, working with our hands, gesturing, writing, keeping active."

Down on Earth, summer gardening gave me my biennial (or so) poison ivy, inspiring Anita to say, "Heaven hath no poisons. There's ivy here, but no one reacts to it. Every kind of injury and disease brings people here. Light bodies stand up to them all."

My last case of poison ivy caught me in the back yard of our second White Meadow Lake home the autumn before I lost Anita. When I was ready to retire, we sold our summer-house, gave notice at our rent controlled Manhattan apartment and moved to a year-round house at the Lake. Anita wouldn't agree to leave New York City until her parents were gone. My happiest retirement memory in the year before she died is a purple sunset slanting into our sun-porch that made Anita say, "You should have made me leave New York sooner."

"Some things light bodies can't do," Anita wrote. "There's no iron pumping, no contact sport, no man-to-man and positively no woman-to-woman grappling. With energy limited, we prefer cerebral to physical activities."

"You know how eyeglasses adjust to the light these days? Nobody wears them here. *The light adjusts to our vision.* However space, light and temperature work on the planets, heaven spoils us. Occupying the same space at the same time, no matter how many we are, everybody fits comfortably."

"The light body rests and sleeps more easily than the bodies we inhabit alive. We never go to bed under pressure. Wait 'til you see what paradise does for your ability to relax, start, stop and change course."

Another night: "Your schedule and mine seldom coincide. My now isn't the same as yours. Besides not having days, hours, minutes and seconds, we have no nights. (The subject confused me as it may you. Heaven's "Now" comes up again.)

When I pressed for specific information about her diet, Anita's response was, "Food-wise, heaven is the no frills aisle of a supermarket. We sip nectar, as much as we want, loaded with light body lubricants. We love the taste, like mocha java, with a light creamy consistency (smoothies?) not thick or fatty. It comes in jugs that need no refrigeration. An unshared jug lasts and lasts or disappears in a meal. Nothing spoils.

"Nectar alone satisfies a light body's needs; but 'solids' appease our souls, memories or both. None of our crackers or breads is made from white flour. We have multi-grain-like breads, rolls, crackers and cookies. Everything stays fresh until it's used.

"(There's) a product like bean curd in several consistencies and flavors, mild and pleasant. There's no meat, causing some new arrivals to make early inquiries about reincarnation. There's no milk. Nothing we consume comes from animals; we're strictly vegetarian. Vegetarians in life love the diet. The rest of us get accustomed to it. Every item is ready to eat. Grains in whatever form, nectar, fruits and vegetables are our staples.

"We eat string beans, beets, carrots, lettuce and other more or less familiar greens. Some, adapted here from planets, were new to me. Our fruit isn't exactly like it is on Earth but reminiscent of it. All fruits and vegetables——all our 'solid' foods provide taste and chewing satisfaction, then turn liquid in 'digestive organs' that are simple intake systems. Nobody eats or drinks more than enough to stoke our working parts."

"We have no silverware or stainless steel cutlery. We use wooden bowls, spoons, knives, forks and ladles. Nothing needs to be sliced, even bread, which we break off the loaf. To restock, I say what I need or write a list before bedtime. Besides nectar, fruit juices, soyessence and tea are on call - no coffee or cocoa. Children have a breadfruit mix that's like cocoa. There's no breadbox. Leftovers don't get stale. They use up.

"We have vegetarian stews and soups. Remember protos 'steak' in Ratner's (a former Lower East Side hearty Hebrew dining shrine)? Our version provides nutritional balance. There's no beef, lamb, pork, or fowl. Fruits, nuts and vegetables are fresh or dried, not canned or frozen. Not as many choices as your Shoprite (still our local supermarket chain in New Jersey), but the ones we have are delicious."

Anita returned again and again to the sensitive matter of food: "If you love heaven you enjoy the diet. We do have occasional surprises. A new item turned up not long back, vanilla pudding!" She reported later that another dinner ration had a chocolatish pudding.

"Soluble solids are grown by very efficient hydroponics. Vat scientists and growers make our diet surprisingly sufficient. Our nectar makes good salad dressing thinned with a little water. Nectar satisfies, but 'solids' are very popular, too.

70

"We don't cook. Our kitchens have keep-warmers that work without fuel. We have wooden pans and light vegetable oils for mixing - by Earth standards a dull diet.

"There are no restaurants. When I have company, I prepare. If I'm visiting, they prepare. Either way, the same food lets us entertain and maintain ourselves physically and socially. Nobody gets indigestion, gas or ulcers."

Work pressure gifted me with years of functional indigestion, but annual medical tests never found an ulcer. At major meetings that we ran, Anita chased me around with a napkin and a chicken leg when I missed meals. We shared a larder of hotel-donated fruit and nuts, sugar-free peanut butter, sugar-free crackers and vegetarian soups, fast food for when there was no time for continental breakfast or to squeeze in lunch or dinner.

"There are no packaged cereals in heaven. Ready-to-eat whole wheat, oats, rice and bran porridges arrive hot or warm from a food commissary, or should I say food Source? Professional chefs and bakers from the planets gravitate there to work.

"Fruit jellies, available in small amounts, are replaced when depleted. Every item's ready to consume. The diet being for consumption without elimination, our desserts liquefy like everything else we eat. I don't know if our new puddings will continue coming. But the sweetness of being here doesn't depend on food."

More: "There are no wheat fields, rice paddies or corn stalks, but their nutrients are in our diet. We eat when and what we please, usually three times a day, getting proper body maintenance the way balanced diets provide it in life.

"Though we don't experience hunger, we do thirst. The all-purpose remedy is pure water. With no bladder or true stomach, you might wonder where everything goes. An internal storage sac retains and breaks down everything we ingest, for circulation to lubrication points, for moisturizing and to provide comfort in this no-atmosphere."

Anita's short summation of paradise: "...sleep-away camp with no war games, always fine weather, relaxation, outings, pleasant get-togethers and all the intellectual stimulation we choose. Reincarnation is not spurred by boredom."

This later: "We have no over-the-counter deli, bakery, appetizing or butcher shops. Animals aren't food; light bodies can't handle animal flesh. Nobody hunts and kills for food or sport."

Manhattan and White Meadow Lake entertaining evenings being fond memories for both of us, Anita wrote, "No halvah here, but I promise you stacks of potato pancakes when you're no longer diabetic."

When Anita had a rented room in San Pedro, one night I loped in from Terminal Island on overnight liberty, smelled something deliciously familiar in the outer hall, burst into her room and discovered her triumphantly adding more to a batch of golden potato pancakes on a

72

platter. I hadn't sunk a tooth into any since leaving New York. Having no stove, Anita fried them on the room's small electric heater. We consumed a mile high stack between us. Navy liberty nights were never sweeter.

"Men and women are about the same height," Anita wrote. "Both sexes here wear light cloth robes at home. We wear sandals if we want to. There's no Shoetown (a defunct northeast shoe chain)."

I asked Anita, "How much more wardrobe do you have? Changes of clothes, Sunday best, what else?"

She answered, "Not much. I do a little wash at home, from habit, not necessity. Light body chemistry leaves no odors and nothing soils. I have one everyday dress and a dressy outfit with a few accessories. They don't wear out. We call everything GI for God Issued. Women dress alike. Men have loincloths and light togas. Nobody struts about nude. Bosoms tuck modestly under our garments.

"Our population doesn't dress for lust or compete for best in show. Dorothy Parker notwithstanding, 'Powder and paint ain't what makes a gal what she ain't' here. Health and heaven are our beauty aids."

Anita's wardrobe in life sounded better to me. She disagreed. "Nobody's plain or glamorous in heaven. You won't be overcome with desire because nothing's done to attract you. No flashing eyes, come-hither looks or low-cut body-tight dresses. We seldom wear our sandals. We have no broken glass, dust, stones or pebbles to walk on."

"We don't float in the air and certainly not in the clouds. But even where there's no grass, walking is good clean fun. The soft loam of our meadows doesn't stick to our feet. Walking is safe and protected.

"This mostly temporary heaven has no time for pursuit. I've yet to see a man or woman lose control. But true love flourishes. Blatant allure isn't what stimulates it.

"We're different in the way we touch, too. "I've never seen it happen but if two people collided here, both would blend a bit, separate, apologize and continue on. I have a better example. When people kiss, their faces literally become one at the lips. I've kissed your Brother Harold, but not his lips. My lips and his cheek meld momentarily. I kissed Cousin Ardo (meet him shortly). Same reaction."

"There's no makeup, eye liner, lip or cheek rouge. No permanent waves. Women wear their hair mostly long and loose. We trim for one another. Many men wear their hair long, too, usually with a headband, but some keep it short, slick or matted. Some have mustaches, some little beards. Nobody's bald. No flowing beards. Men don't shave close. They usually have light soft fuzz on their faces."

"Men have light outdoor robes, too. I told you about womens' all-alike dresses, modest at the bodice, with no bosom accent. If we want, we wear hair bands or ribbons. If not, it hangs loose neatly, like mine."

A note on communications: "No tape recorders here, Or CD's. If you could bring one, there's no place to plug it in and we have no batteries. Radio doesn't come from radio sets, it just comes - reaching everywhere in heaven.

"There are no commercials, just information – not in rounded, pearly annoucerspeak – just plain talk, any language we need to hear it in. Afterlife is underplayed - its gentle, omnipresent aura stimulates us without pressure or guilt."

When I asked about sex, Anita explained, "Light bodies blend, Daddy says, in a rewarding, refreshing way. There's plenty of casual socializing but no stalking, harassment or rape. Single people find each other. What they do is between them. Heaven isn't a monastery or nunnery." She also told me, "There's no prostitution but a good amount of discreet free love, as it used to be called. Our residences provide privacy."

"When people mate here, there's no ceremony. They commit to each other and live together. Marriages usually succeed and lead to double reincarnation. But if a marriage doesn't work out, the couple part on friendly terms, both free to try again.

"Nobody is consumed by passion. The physical part is muted because of the lack of 'too, too solid' sex organs in light bodies. Our love will rekindle itself - and here, as everywhere, lovemaking matters. There are lots of eligible mates here; but if we have loving living mates, we wait for them. There's no temptation."

"Sometimes you worry that I'm not real because I approve of your dating. I wouldn't have in life, Buster. Laissez faire makes more sense here than on the planets. We have no celestial ménages a trois. There are no preachments against it and consenting humans aren't criticized or ostracized for their choices.

"Heavenly sex is really deep cuddling. Though light bodies *have* no unnecessary organs, we love, laugh, enjoy and are satisfied. It was never intended for so important an expression of love as lovemaking not to be part of living here. There's an emotional climax but no light body acquires or produces chemicals promoting offspring.

"I get all this intelligence from your father-in-law, who s always happy to supply it. He says there are lots of ways to make love. Daddy would go into it but I prefer us to find out for ourselves."

"Classes and lectures about sex are fascinating. We hear about our world and others. Unlike on Earth, or should I say in earthly TV, movies and popular books, we don't need or miss traditional sex. I don't know if that will be a relief to you or not."

Sometimes I get her answers to unspoken questions on my mind. One night Anita said, "Sex nearly always interested you more than me. Discovering that almost everything I did or said turned you on taught me to be loving but not too encouraging - or I'd have spent forty-seven years in bed."

"You've found a loving life after I died. (You'll catch up with that later on.) Lots of men don't wait for their wives to die. But you did." It was too true. Over the years, when a woman looked good to me, I ran away. For me, it was unthinkable to cheat – well, occasionally thinkable but not doable.

Anita twitted me when I asked if she knew how the sex race was fixed for a selected sperm cell to attach itself to a particular ovum. "Are you being scientifically curious or prurient? Optimally, the selected sperm and ovum produce an assigned human embryo. Misfires are erased by natural or induced abortions."

"You understand why nobody conceives or gives birth here. Enough population passes through without added local traffic, which explains heaven's absence of wombs, penises or your ever-popular sperm races. Passion is for planets. Pleasure without passion is heaven. We have, however, a degree of sexual pleasure in our infertile paradise.

"Absent reproductive urge, what's left is civilized love-making agreeable for both sexes. Days here are unnamed and unnumbered. It doesn't matter when two people make love. When there's stimulus – and there is - it never gets out of hand. We have no intemperate or forced alliances, only affectionate coupling of consenting participants."

"I've read that many pregnancies aren't cocktails from heaven at all but spontaneous human combustion or forced penetration. The average number of planetary births without divine supervision is 12%. But all become part of God's human family."

I pursued the subject further. "You say light bodies have no unnecessary organs. Does that really mean no sexual organs?"

"You've got it - but don't despair. Pleasure isn't absent, just plumbing."

I didn't despair. Our letters were a constant source of joy. Anita said they were for her, too. She wrote, "Doing our letters, I feel our hands are joined and we're walking together where there's only our space, our love and us."

"We race in cloudy warmth when we wish ourselves from hither to thither; but even a *light* body has too much substance to float aimlessly. Decorative clouds provide shade and never form cold or warm weather fronts, thunderstorms or heavy rains.

"Dew and mist keep green things green, flowers fragrant and air healthy. Walking in mist is bracing. Not enough of it's done. Most people just whoosh."

In a subsequent letter, Anita amended that comment.. "The inefficiency of walking when you can whisk is apparent after a while. So we stop walking, which uses energy, and whisk, which doesn't. There's no health cost to not walking. Light bodies don't deteriorate for being cloud potatoes. Exercise freaks continue their habits until they settle for heaven's less strenuous perks. Heavy exercises are no problem but we have better things to do with timelessness than body building. We never binge, either. We use food to oil our parts and pay no attention to calories, carbohydrates, fats and protein."

"Are you weightless?" I asked.

She answered, "We're lighter but not weightless. The atmosphere is controlled to support light bodies. We have no barometric pressure. Without it to resist we don't acquire pressure-resistant bulk." Soon after, she wrote something she learned in the library, that light bodies are about six-tenths the density of Earth humans. "That's higher than on some planets, sparser than on others."

81

In another letter, "I understand the Force we call God and that some people here believe is Jesus Christ. They say Jesus is here, but he isn't seen here except in fancy. He may *be* the Son of God or simply have been an exceptional human being for his time."

Anita and I know that many readers have their own strong views on religion, especially the one they have embraced. This book has its point of view but isn't intended to intrude on yours. Who's right will always be argued on the planets. An example is an old joke my father told in his indelible Irish brogue:

PATTY: We're the ones who can brag. Did any of you Jews ever make Pope?"

ABIE: No, but one of *our* boys made God!

The point is, what we have to do is live with our differences and let live, believe and let believe.

Anita wrote, "Christians say Jesus *is* God or His son or both. Our people don't believe he's God but that what he tried to accomplish probably earned him a special place here." (There's more about Jesus later in the book.)

About study: "Learning here comes from reading and lectures, after which students challenge politely or ask questions. Group study analyzes, weighs and often, but not always, reaches consensus.

"Religions, ethics and behavior get big attention; courses try to define what's civilized, what we owe each other - and respect, not tolerance, for our differences."

In the Fifties the Brotherhood Synagogue shared a sanctuary with a Christian denomination in the East Village. Anita and I joined when Dody, smitten with our unmarried Rabbi Bloch, took religious instruction for her bat mitzvah, a girl's induction to the Jewish fold. After Sabbath services, we put away Hebrew bibles and prayer shawls to make way for our Christian brothers' and sisters' Sunday services. Anita loved the experience. But Dody lost interest (the rabbi got married) and we were ready to move uptown to the West Side. We dropped our membership.

Anita's letters from heaven were and are a blissful blend of love, happy memories and forecasts for us when my life ends. I pressed her for specifics on everything about heaven until it got it through to me that she could respond only as fast as she learned.

Anita didn't have to ask about my life without her. She heard me gripe in our letters and sits in on my doctors' appointments by keeping our channel "on low," as she puts it. She knows the ups and down of my blood glucose, knows when I'm chipper or dilapidated, when my heart's working with me or against me, makes light of my arthritis, neuropathy, lightheaded spells, weakening eyesight – and isn't above giving medical advice. I love it - makes me feel wanted.

83

I missed her terribly, puttering around an empty house, learning computer, eating alone, visiting my daughters, family and friends, feeling angry and sorry for myself, trying to write, and trying to forget – without enthusiasm until our channeling began. Learning how much better off Anita is than I was, I had moments when joining her any way I could seemed like a great idea. But she told me to stay at it even before we cooked up the idea of doing this book.

Anita continued about life in heaven: "Study's easy and pleasant. There are no distractions or grades. We stay on subject easily. We discuss human betterment often. Our intellectuals are patient with people who aren't as smart as they are and vice versa."

Religion came up often. She accused, "You gave me the attitude that organized religions are all businesses perpetuating themselves at the expense of believers. Clergies *have* perverted religious history and tailored their teaching to their agendas. Major religions once taught that humans die and reincarnate. They don't mention it now. They promote the concept of heaven as a reward for faithfully following what *they* teach; instilling fear in people – of going to hell for deviating.

"The devout and unbelievers alike open their hearts and minds here. Not forced to love God, we do because we're inspired to, not because a bible says we have to or else."

Then: "Your Sister Doris has decided to go back to earth for another life. She has been instructed in reincarnation and has chosen her new family. When

84

you hear that, you have to ask yourself who'd pick Africa or *any* place there's starvation? Yet infants born every day in those places starve. Did they *choose* such lives? I'll try to learn more."

Doris, middle child of the five Ober siblings, one girl with four brothers, bright, forthright and a budding sculptor, never had a sick day until February 1937 when she died at 21 after thirty-six hours of raging influenza/pneumonia. Visiting a sick friend, Doris came home, got sick, lacked resistance and died in Boston's Beth Israel Hospital. Until that day, death never touched our family. Now I'm Mike and Gussie's only one left.

In another letter, Anita channeled this, written before she learned that there are ten universes, each originally with one peopled planet: "There *is* life elsewhere, not just on Earth. I meet people from other planets who think as we do, speak of things we don't know about and appear brighter - but I don't know if they're superior to all of us or just smarter than I am. Norm, these people aren't reptiles or weird aliens imagined in Earth films. They're more *like* us than different.

"They come from places like Antrusia, Boronok...no, with a c... and Telentek."

"As you and I probably will when we decide to, most transients here reincarnate to where they came from. Some, after study or, just for the heaven of it, decide to start over in a new place. Others elect to switch sexes from one life to the next."

"I understand that we remember everything important in previous lives subconsciously. But each new life cleans the slate of the conscious mind."

"The more I see 'aliens,' the less different they seem. Their languages are not incomprehensible by telepathy, but some have learned English, French, German and other languages of Earth. They study them here if they're interested in Earth locations for their next lives. For those that pick alien planets, their languages are taught here, too."

Anita and I never discussed moving to other worlds. Nor did we plan to share new lives on Earth. Instead, we decided together to take a different direction, as you will see.

This subject comes up again when there's more information about Jesus. Mentions of telepathy that follow continue to reveal the extraordinary communication value of this phenomenon of heaven.

"When we talk here to people from other planets, they speak in their languages and we understand in ours. We ask questions in our language. They answer in theirs and we understand each other. Heaven is no Babel. In public places we mix and mingle freely through heaven's automatic translation service."

It took me a while to grasp what Anita meant by this miracle. What it comes down to is that heaven's telepathy automatically translates any language into the language you know best, when reading a book, hearing a lecture, listening to the radio, watching entertainment or just talking with someone who doesn't speak your language.

"Thought exchanging," Anita insists, "is a more honest way of dealing with one another than speaking out loud. Spoken words are censored by the brain and ego. Exchanged thoughts are instinctive, without motive and embellishment. Exchanged thoughts that overlap each other sort themselves out. Try that with audible words when two people talk at once."

Anita and I attended an Ober Family reunion in Boston where everyone talked at once and nobody finished a sentence or managed to make a whole point. She used to say of our Boston visits that I took her there to die, alluding to her dread, shared by her sisters-in-law, of even short visits with Gussie. The family reunion was where Anita met and fell in love with my Uncle Sam Corwin, our dear, gentle-spoken patriarch who lived to 110 and departed life peacefully with his mental motor in high gear to the end.

"Telepathic networking," Anita concluded, makes appointments easy to make, keep or postpone. We really appreciate its great contribution to afterlife."

She digressed. "When you edit our copy I'm usually tuned in. *If I see something I expressed badly, I correct it through your brain.* You can't tell my edits from yours, but if anything you write down changes a fact, *I change it right back.*"

More on telepathy, "When we communicate by it, we don't need to say hello, is this whoever? Telepathy never gets a wrong number. Wherever we or they are, it finds whoever we want to talk to. In turn, we both know who is calling.

"We have no telephones or answering machines. The called party gets the message - delayed if he's been away. When we say we'll call, we mean telepathically."

I asked Anita what she did about a call in the middle of work she couldn't leave.

"Answer it. If I'm that busy I promise to get back as soon as I can. If the call can't wait – which is almost never – I give it priority and what I'm doing waits."

I wondered if she ever tried talking to God telepathically. "We talk to God often – some of us very often. He doesn't answer. Lots here claim telepathic answers from God. Maybe they think so. I can't picture Him waiting for my questions or advice and He's too busy for an invitation to drop over and have nectar with the family."

Anita wrote on how heaven's residents interact without time as a guide. "When I want to see Mother and Daddy, telepathic outreach usually gets a fast response. If they're busy, they suggest, 'We'll call you when we're free' - 'Come next snack' - 'After the concert' – whatever. When we agree to meet, arrival is usually immediate."

Later this: "Heaven is like the Speaker's Corner at the Marble Arch (in London). Anyone can stand on a figurative soapbox here and opinionate as far as voice – or telepathy - can carry. Nobody objects, nobody argues and sometimes nobody listens."

Finally on telepathy: "After comparative religion and meditation classes the next most popular course is telepathy - how to make contact with a loved one - and use of automatic writing for doing what we're doing now. If we keep writing, God willing, we may help others find the way to *their* lost loved ones, which would be heaven plus."

PART THREE

One day in 1943, during WWII in Sullivans Auditorium, Sampson Naval Training Station near Geneva, New York - where I used an office to write the base's radio programs, Anita's father phoned me from Manhattan. He was incoherent with grief, but I finally understood that he wanted me to tell Anita as gently as possible that her favorite Cousin, Arnold Lipkin, an Air Force pilot, had been killed taking off over the New Hebrides. Abe identified Arnold by providing plaster casts of his dental work.

That evening after dinner, I drew Anita closer in our enchanted cottage and told her. She didn't cry but her tears flowed for hours. Then, for the rest of the night Anita talked to me about growing up with Arnold, who protected her from summer camp stallions - "More than I wanted him to"- what a dedicated student he was and his decision to volunteer for pilot training in the Army Air Force – to be responsible for his own life, not become a victim of someone else's mistakes.

From heaven Anita channeled, "Arnold's parents Ida and Iz never brought it up, but he's been in repair since his awful accident, in a laboratory where destroyed souls are rebuilt. Ida and Iz weren't too hopeful until they got word he'd be joining them soon.

"When you're consumed by an explosion, repair's a longer process than starting out as chemistry and being born. But Ida and Iz were told that, in his light body, he'd be as he was alive, in his mid-twenties, undamaged, no scars or pain, like the rest of us.

"A scientist doing gene restoration says war can destroy souls totally, the way peacetime explosions or accidents can. When sick people die we say, 'At least his suffering is over.' We can't conceive of people who die the way Ardo (Arnold) did."

Somewhat later: "So now, Norman, you're wondering how my soul survived cremation, if it took so long to fix Arnold's. My soul was liberated when I died. Arnold's was demolished too quickly for rescue."

Later: "Ardo is going to join us soon. Ida and Iz saw him. He's the way they remember him, speaks the same, *is* the same Brooklyn boy who went to war and never came back. They told him I'm here. He was shocked until Ida mentioned that I was seventy years old when I died and he would have been two years older if he'd lived."

A month or so after that, when I expected Anita to describe the first peopled planet, she channeled instead, "I've been busting to tell you! Arnold's with us, looking exactly as I remember him. He's amused that both of us are the same age as when he left for the Air Force. He also says I'm beautiful. They fixed his eyes fine!

"Scientists who recreated his soul told him restoring a body is no problem (they fit him for a light body) - but repairing a soul involves exact gene reconstruction. He was unconscious during rebuilding. They brought him out of it near the end of the process.

"When he heard that normal brain function is hard to restore, he took inventory of himself and decided they did well enough. He's pleased to be with his parents, but will acquaint himself with opportunities here and decide whether to reincarnate or stay. Ida and Iz will do what Arnold does. Uncle Iz asked at Reincarnation what they could do to stay together as a family."

Anita wrote that Arnold, after whooshing among the sights of heaven, told her about an overlook where he saw the inhabited planets in each universe. "Arnold says, when you look down at them, it's clear why planet people can't cross over to each other.

"Any universe can be scoped by equipment here. Shifts of a few dozen observers monitor what's happening in different parts of each peopled planet. Arnold says it's easy (at the platform) to see how vast space complicates fixing things that go wrong on the planets. That backs up what I've been telling you – control is limited.

"Observers are more than watchers. Arnold says visualization headgear focuses where their minds direct and they make oral observations to a recording device."

Anita mentioned Arnold saying that, after perishing in his plane he was reconstituted because of good character. "The long, difficult process isn't used for souls of wrongdoers' bodies - an exception to God's law of return!

"Arnold is inclined now to find a place for himself here in sciences that study the planets and probe space. He says restoring him was creation without a

93

host mother. This form of reproduction, being improved all the time, interests Arnold who, slob that he is, says he has no quarrel with the old way, intercourse."

Arnold and I would have liked each other. Learning that girls were packaged differently from boys, like him I had to wait long years to experience the difference. In Puritan Boston in the 1930's, girls wanted to get married, if not first, then definitely before a replay; a dilemma for my Brother Harold and me in our late teens.

The next night, Anita reported that Arnold had taken her to the platform that oversees the universes. "I stood there and held a protective post because it's scary. That was silly. If I fell off, I'd whoosh myself back up.

"I looked into the 'tops' of each universe. There's so much space in each of them! Black bands separating them defeat crossing over. A rocket flying around the perimeters of its universe won't get through the magnetized fields that seal them off from one another. I learned that from one of the planet watchers.

"It's awesome looking into each universe, see*ing* there are stars, planets, solar systems, and, in each, one planet with human life, where pulses beat, minds work, bodies function and interact, - except for one planet named Enistor that lost its people."

Later: "Arnold has decided not to attach himself here after all. He's thinking of reincarnating to Earth. Ida and Iz have asked about opportunities to return as triplets.

"They want to live around Sheepshead Bay (Brooklyn), where they had their happiest years. They want to share life with Arnold and can't do it any other way." Arnold's younger Brother Walter, retired, lives in Florida at this writing.

The Lipkins eventually reincarnated as triplets, getting their wish. Somewhere along Brooklyn's Atlantic seashore, Anita and I like to think, Ida, Iz and Arnold have been welcomed to a good home by loving parents and their families."

That brings us to one of heaven's mundane miracles, living quarters: "Houses are 'light homes.' Self-expanding frames, walls and inner space are fourth dimension functions I can't explain. Home space isn't rigid as in life. That's not a joke. Also, housing doesn't expand by ones. Whole neighborhoods appear shortly before 'tenants' show up to occupy them. I've seen that happen more than once.

"When there's a sudden need, basic homes stack one above the other, three stories, if necessary. Nobody climbs stairs. Up and down locomotion, entry and exit are willed. I've slept in a single story home and wakened a level or two higher.

Stuyvesant Town had inflexible dimensions and rules. If we had a boy and a girl, we could have gotten a third bedroom. But the only way Anita and I could have separate bedrooms for our two girls was to move into a big West Side apartment at 124 West 79th Street, where Dody, Amy and our marriage flourished. As Dody and Amy grew, huge rooms were a great benefit, especially the large l-shaped reception, dining and living room complex where Anita and her exclusive dishwasher presided over social events.

"Heaven's living rooms are moderately spacious. They have dining areas with efficiency kitchen counters where our food arrives ready-to-eat from our magic commissary. There's a bedroom, more if needed. We're never crowded. Space grows or shrinks according to the number and needs of its occupants.

"Couples share a bedroom. Children reared to median age get their own. The basic living area grows, but needs no extra space - fourth-dimension architecture!

"Light furniture is very comfortable. A sofa by day is a bed at night. The form of a chair responds to need and use. Discovery that our furniture adapts to our changing needs is quite a surprise at first."

*Two and a half years after I left the Navy, with housing still hard to find in Manhattan, we broke out of the Rosenblums' living room and moved to Stuyvesant Town; kitchen, living room, dining area, one bath, one bedroom and no closet doors for years. Anita and I couldn't have been happier. Our government subsidized rent was, I think, $63 a month, including utilities. Anita said, "My poor parents are so relieved." We were, too, until the new sectional sofa arrived, four **big** pieces. Anita joyously slid them into place and burst into tears. The sofa swallowed our living room. Her mother and father raced down by cab. I rushed home from CBS. Lily, bless her, saved our marriage and Anita's sanity by figuring out how and where the pieces could be placed without the room looking like a furniture warehouse. Abe and I pushed furniture as directed.*

Anita channeled further, "Heaven's homes don't have shades. Windows have no panes, only eye level openings. Our temperature is never actually hot or cold.

"We have few belongings, no files or filing cabinets. Nothing needs refrigeration. With no physical functions, we have no toilets. Heaven's an uncomplicated place."

Anita told me more about her home in our first truly legible letter, printed from my computer. "Anticipating us being together, I have a double with a
queen-sized bed. No chintz curtains, I'm afraid.

That recalled a crisp cheery set she sewed for our cottage in Sampson Naval Station,
where we reveled in each other for six months before moving on. During our four day honeymoon
we had stayed at the Barbizon Plaza Hotel facing Central Park South, saw Broadway shows,
dined at great Manhattan restaurants and made glorious love. Then I drove a borrowed half-ton
panel truck to Sampson with Anita and our belongings. During the drive, we were stopped three
times by highway police, who had to see for themselves what a crazy happy sailor and the
blushing girl he had with him were doing in a panel truck marked MARIONETTE GUILD.
After they read my leave orders, they wished us luck. They loved her. Who didn't?

When I wasn't on Navy duty, we took long walks, picked fruit in abandoned orchards
and held hands crossing former farmlands - Anita used to say, "Like two little children." The
area completely taken over by Uncle Sam, Sampson's vacant acreage was our private larder
where my newlywife cried at the sight of a small old family graveyard with, "...so many so
young."

Back to Anita's letters and these short tidbits about everyday heaven:
"Cloth drapes are available for decoration and, I suppose, for a touch of
individuality. Our drapes and furnishings are GI. Rich or poor when alive,
nobody's home is much different from anyone else's and nobody cares. God is felt
in everything here though seldom seen (as He will be) within his cloud cocoon."

"There is, as I wrote, a large living room with counter space that passes for a kitchen. There are no electrical or gas appliances, just the counter with its wooden dishes, bowls and wooden GI 'cutlery.'"

"You and I won't have to move when you come – our home will grow as we need it to and house us comfortably." Later she writes that it did expand and denied that was a hint for me to start packing. "By the way, a light bed is a cloud that supports our weight. Sheets and blankets are unnecessary. Temperature adjusts itself to taste. Chairs and sofas are cloud-formed, of sufficient strength to hold us comfy."

"Single adults who prefer them have their own places. Couples share larger quarters. Infants and children live with related or adoptive families, with extra rooms added. At the median age or sooner, they move out on their own. When single adults marry here, they decide which gives up a home and the other's expands for them".

"People who prefer their own sex share homes, too. Gays and lesbians raise no eyebrows and are slower to reincarnate than others because nobody objects to them here."

"If a visitor brings a musical instrument to a home party, he or she plays for the crowd. Musicians practice as they did in life. Professional players are artistic, unpaid professionals here. Invite around and you can get a trio or quartet. Symphony orchestras perform in concert halls that accommodate all audience sizes."

Her next letter was earthier. "My housekeeping days are over. We live in less work for mother homes. Nothing we wear gets grungy; clothes need no sewing, repair or discarding. Summer or winter, such as they are, clothes and bedclothes stay clean."

"If anything spills it disappears. There's no plumbing or running water. If you need water your pitcher fills up. Housekeeping has new meaning."

"When families arrive together, they start out living together. Older adults grow young, their children get older until they're equal in age right up to reincarnation."

I asked why Anita didn't live with her folks: "*You're* why. I have *our* place."

I inveighed, "Good. Please don't marry. I don't want to evict a stranger."

"Did I tell you not to marry? Sauce for the Bullo is sauce for the Bulless." I being Taurus, she, in heaven, and Dody and Amy on Earth call me Bullo pretty often.

More about heaven's housing. "I'm in one of sixty units. I don't know where they go when they're empty; probably deflated and stored on shelves."

"Neighbors sometimes say goodbye before reincarnating - not always. Homes they vacate need no painting or fumigating. Their houses, furniture and utensils go to new occupants. We move to new units when ours lose most of their people. Later, an entirely new neighborhood may appear at the same place, ready for occupancy."

I questioned, "Do furnishings move with them?"

Anita's answer: "Yes, as if by magic. Housing units are thick white cloud blocks you can't see through. Beds seem small until you occupy them. My section houses widows (I'm considered one), some unmarried and divorced women, no families. Our unit has women from Earth. People from other planets have theirs. Once mental telepathy kicks in, migrants from all planets are able to socialize. There are no color lines. With light bodies you can't tell one skin color from another anyway."

Skin color mattered to Anita's grandmother, Mahmah. In her nineties, sharp as a tack, the old lady took me aside for a little chat during one of our pre-Navy visits to Brooklyn. Anita's suntan was flourishing that summer. Mahmah instructed me, I supposed, to make sure I knew my girl friend wasn't colored, "Look on her palms. She's a vhite goil." Mahmah lived into her middle nineties, wise, funny and adorable.

Back to channeling, I asked Anita what street she lived on in heaven. She said, "We have no street names. We think ourselves to where we need to go and we're there. Or we think home and we're there. We don't think addresses, just destinations."

I always wanted more details. "What does your home look like, besides being made of clouds? Is there a porch? Wooden floors? Are your walls clouds?"

"Heaven's our porch. We have no doors or full windows. Walls, roof and floors are hard fabric. No skyscrapers, apartment complexes, buses, streetcars or automobiles. We walk if we want, and visualize ourselves to and from further points."

Anita mentioned detaching earlier. I was curious to know how it worked. "When it comes to revisiting scenes of my immediate past life – the only past one we here *can* revisit, by the way – it's like checking out of a hotel. We don't need permission but we don't flit off without first detaching from and checking our light bodies.

"When that's done we're ready to go, soul only, disembodied as when we arrived here. While we're away - maximum period is about fifteen of your hours - our light bodies are tuned up and held until we return. It's that simple. We revisit when and where we choose, then check back in when we should. If we want to be away longer, we get more time by returning to heaven and checking out again. It takes no time at all."

If that miracle were available on Earth, it would have been a bonanza when Anita and I flew to and from potential meeting sites and to and from meetings our embattled group arranged for a baker's dozen years. We loved flying to new destinations, less so staging the large meetings that stressed me to a frazzle, worried Anita for my health and sparked our worst arguments over my explosive outbursts of exasperation.

I asked Anita why there was a time limit for detaching. She explained that, if overzealous spirits visiting loved ones of the last life outstayed their energy reserves, they'd lose power to return and help would have to be dispatched to rescue them. "It doesn't happen often but it happens.

"If I detach to visit a theatre on my own, unlike when I see a show through our channel and your mind, I reach my own conclusions. Experiencing events through you pleases me and doesn't start the clock on my energy, but your mindset gets in my way."

This from a later letter: "I sometimes use pre-nap periods to visit you or the girls. I detach to Boulder, too, and indulge in an occasional look at Timothy (our grandson, who was then in college and is, at this writing, is a new father of three)."

"Most peopled planets have forms of TV, stages, concert halls and arenas. Musicians from all worlds, composers famous where they came from play new music here. We enjoy pieces Beethoven and Mozart composed after their last lifetimes. We have books Victor Hugo and Alexander Dumas wrote after they died - there are scores of other great writers, composers and performers from Earth and other planets."

"Nobody wears wings and plays a harp; though harp is featured in orchestras. Concerts are wonderful. We have had Leonard Bernstein, Koussevitsky and Rachmaninoff, to name-drop only three. They performed their favorites from life and introduced new works." Anita's heaven sounded better all the time.

She had another piece of information: "I don't know the source of our water, but we never lack it and our greenery never withers. Leaves don't fall. Grass grows a few inches and stops.

"For exercise and sport, people push objects with toothless wooden rakes, hurl javelins, and toss weights, quoits or mock horseshoes. Horses aren't shod or ridden. Unbroken, they race over grassy plains, running free until they're reincarnated.

"We have playing cards. Our families still enjoy bridge, whist, rummy, canasta, poker and other old favorites. People of other planets have their card games. Youngsters do every kind of hopping game you can imagine and some you can't. One I've watched, called skipaway, is for alternate jumping and jogging races on rounded pathways.

"There's no junk lying around heaven, but shops provide craft materials free, chipped from universal space debris, drawn off in programs to keep travel and communication routes relatively unobstructed. Artisans rummage in the shops for beads, bits, pieces and scrap, including cured glass sheets that end up in all kinds of novelties."

On sports: "We have hand and bat ball, but no ice skating or games like ice hockey, boxing, wrestling, football and soccer that can inflict pain and injury. There are ponds and lakes to play and swim in but no oceans anywhere. Every housing area has a large pool in its own park with places to picnic, and paths and trails to walk on. We live simply and enjoy everything there is in our gracious environs."

That brings to mind the lush wooded acres of West Point Farms, Central Valley, New York. Our family were casual diners there who became loving mutual friends of the owners, Barbara and Henri Apisson. Dody and Amy were the dumplings of their eyes. Amy's middle name, Laurel, came from the graceful shrubs abundant along the resort's wooded walks. Our spirits thrived on Barbara and Henri's hospitality and love. Barbara's mid-east culinary expertise and my volunteered public relations services brought them more than a decade of diners who appreciated their excellent cuisine. Anita and I helped serve others when they were "stuck."

Elizabeth Kremb, their undemonstrative German housekeeper, was assistant chef and loyal vassal to Barbara. We adored them all and spent many privileged weekends as their guests.

Back to our letters: "Daddy's come across games never heard of on Earth, brought here by people from other planets. Sports events are sometimes organized in memory of remembered athletic heroes on every planet of origin."

Anita remembered omitting tennis when she listed local sports. "We play as we did. Other people play differently. In one variation, balls are bashed at the net, the object being to drive them through pre-cut holes, scoring points when they're not hit back.

"There are foot parades with no floats. Participants recite, sing or chant to music accompanied by instruments familiar and unfamiliar - woodwinds, for instance - different from any I've ever seen that trap and release air to produce harmonic tones."

The next night Anita asked me to read back our last letter. When I did, she added this: "Artisans who built musical instruments in life craft them here. Some have weird shapes, piping and keyboards producing beautiful sounds. Some instruments do what violins, bass fiddles and cellos do, without strings or bows. Artists finger open areas in boxes that resonate vibrations pleasing to the ear. There are no phonographs, records, tapes or discs, just live music."

Quick question: "How is your music presented?"

Quick answer: "We will and whoosh ourselves to concerts. We also get musical entertainment at home. A celestial 'Muzak' library lets us pick titles. I want a particular vocal? It plays. Almost any popular song or classical aria - we get what we want. Any orchestration, tempo or arrangement - we get it."

"What does it all play on?"

"Play *in*. Inside our heads with superb quality."

"If there's rock and roll, I don't hear it. I could eavesdrop on what clusters of youngsters listen to." She never said she did and I never pushed it.

"Besides concerts we have theatre, ballet, fine arts and no end of cultural activity. If there's TV, I don't know where." It turns up later. "Ubiquitous radio announcements give us details on events to attend or to order up at home.

"Entertainment is available at what I call Miracle Mile. We don't *have* to go to shows there; we can 'see' them by calling them in. Groups either go or 'attend' at someone's home. Either way, at curtain time we're 'seated' and every seat's the best in the house. Nobody's behind a post or too far away to hear and see.

"*You* walk, ride, drive or fly. We whoosh or walk. Too much sitting leads *you* to atrophy, not us. Life's wonderful, our climate so perfect that even I don't miss ocean cruises, excursions to the mountains or my revered ocean beaches."

Every summer, all summer long at White Meadow Lake, Anita had her own corner on Beach #2, soaking up the sun, surrounded by the women in our clique by day and the husbands, too, in the evening. Our children were in and around the water in droves. We picnicked on the beach and ate food delivered by suppliers on U.S. Route 46 in Denville and Rockaway. Anita

108

was supremely contented there summers. She always called her corner of Beach #2 The Store. Summer life, for her, was heaven on earth.

Anita reported that heaven has numerous lush rolling landscapes, indescribably beautiful slopes, valleys, broad blue lakes and river basins reached by mental trekking – or by doing it the hard way, hiking.

"Here we will our way to exotic destinations we hear about from others. I seldom wander far. I expect you'll reawaken my wanderlust with your appetite for travel. There are dozens of interesting places, but I like to be close to home and work where I can keep my telepathic eye on you.

"Nothing's rushed. You *never* see anyone run. There are no emergencies. Nobody would think of elbowing someone else. People move about with natural grace when walking – almost a glide.

"When whooshing about, we don't see or feel others flit past. If I want to go to the library, which is a distance, I will it and I'm there. There's no sensation of being whisked. *You* can't will yourself aboard an airplane and across the country. *You* have to buy tickets and walk or climb aboard. You know when you're airborne. We don't feel it."

Speaking of airplanes, I began one letter to Anita on paper, aboard the shuttle to Boston just before takeoff. The hourlong hop was notable for showing us we could channel during flight. As we moved into takeoff position, Anita marveled, "Engine vibrations don't drown us out. Our channel penetrates metal, buildings and solid walls. Airborne, *you* can't hear the plane's loud speaker, but nothing overrides us."

One Oscar night on television, I turned the set off early to do our letter. I asked Anita, who enjoyed watching the Oscars, "If I leave the set turned on when I'm not watching, can you enjoy the show if you want to?"

Her answer was, "No, darling. I see stage shows you go to through your eyes and mind set. It's the same for movies and TV."

That night we had another joust over the concept that now is the permanent natural state in heaven. "I keep gagging at the idea that time never passes there. Do you mean it passes but nobody cares?"

Anita answered, "That's not what I mean. Don't try to make heaven fit your concept of time. Heaven has no commerce or industry, no planes or trains to catch, no dates under the Astor clock (an old Times Square meeting place), no clocks anywhere."

On one of our early dates, Anita and I agreed to meet at the Astor clock to have dinner at the hotel, which was located in Times Square. She was a wraith in brown wearing her mink stole and matching fur hat she made from fur left over when her mother had her mink coat shortened. Considering how little I earned back then, instead of the Astor, we should have found ourselves a street vendor and had hot sweet potatoes.

I kept bringing up *now* in heaven: "What about entertainment, lectures and group and committee meetings? Without a set time, how do you know when to meet?"

110

"We *know*. If we don't we check by telepathy. Getting anywhere here is instantaneous. We get where we're supposed to and there's always room."

I tried another tack. "But it doesn't make sense. Our tomorrow becomes today, then yesterday. Why not heaven's?"

"A feature of God's love is pressure-free timelessness in a haven from rain, snow, sleet, hot or cold spells and from your obsession with time. *H*eaven nourishes the soul, restores the mind and wakens the spirit, all *now*, undiluted by *and then*."

Anita added patiently, "I'd have forgotten how to think in Earth time if you didn't refer to it so often. Planetary people keep track of time in many different ways. Having no time here avoids confusion for everyone from everywhere.

"Heaven is a blessed interregnum that invigorates our souls, minds and imaginations. Besides being time-free here, we have no day names, no mornings, afternoons or evenings. It's either now, not now, once, before, soon, later – but no tomorrow, next week or a week from Sunday.

"Enistor," (the first populated planet – Anita explains in Enistor's chapter why it's not peopled any more) "had the same time system heaven used to for thousands of years. But when other universes started sending souls to heaven, confusion keeping time was chaotic until God decided that measuring it here was more trouble than it was worth."

111

"Since our population comes from nine (formerly ten) different time systems and most of us reincarnate to our planets of origin, why impose a different system here to muddy the collective unconscious? Once back in life, we relearn time easily, already subconsciously accustomed to it. Nothing we do here depends on time. Absence of now is impossible in tick-tock societies. The planets can't escape the clock without upsetting business, commerce and even pleasure."

I digested that and changed the subject, "Do you go out on the town often? When and where are your plays and lectures? And *television?* I thought there was none."

She explained. "Turns out we have it. It's a minor item at entertainment centers. We go there when we want to run with a pack – to classes, too. Humor from entertainment centers and education from classrooms come to us at home, if we like. Most of us watch the educational programs, even the ones for precocious children, the only kind we have here."

Both our daughters were precocious. Dody passed her test for admission to Hunter College Elementary School for gifted children. The funny part of it was that Dody took the test only to accompany her friend Lisa when she took hers. Lisa didn't make it, fanning cool air on Anita's friendship with her mother. Later, with no fanfare, quiet Amy beat Dody's 99th percentile rating by a tenth of a percent. Anita was much more restrained in her enthusiasm than I was.

Education in heaven: "It isn't compulsory here but nobody wants or has to be a dummy. We don't need volumes or visual aids – just the brain's on-off switch and a course selector. There are four course choices at all times. Whichever language lecturers choose, we hear them in languages we understand.

I asked, "Education doesn't bore you?"

She reminded me, "Boring doesn't describe any aspect of life here. Picture a world of idealistic Boy and Girl Scouts. We're such a population. Lots of our upbeat and affirmative stage plays would die on Broadway, but we adore them."

I took the cue: "Do Broadway plays and musicals have professsional casts?"

Anita replied, "We sure do. Dramas are particularly popular. Bad guys get belly laughs but they aren't booed. It's not done. We go to the performances or watch at home.

"Performers, like lecturers, speak in languages they know and we hear them in ours. No librettos necessary – we hear operas, too, in our own languages. Music choices range from solo performances to symphony orchestras – with every size group in between. I love quartets, quintets and sextets, playing what you, bad boy, used to call chamber pot music."

"Conversation's the main ingredient at social occasions. There's no alcohol. Everywhere arguments are mild. Londonish Speakers' Corners are all over the place."

Doing another letter, we tried again to see if I could convey my thoughts to Anita's mind by telepathy as she did hers to mine. She suggested, "Stop writing and just think something. If I sense your message I'll say it back."

I cast an unspoken thought her way. Anita reported, "I have most of your message. I scribbled so fast, I need time to read it." She started to propose that we discuss it in our next letter and then saw that what she had was gibberish.

"The first sentence makes no sense." There couldn't have been much more than a sentence. "Let's try again, slower - try to ease into it." We tried again. No luck.

Some time later we found we could swap unwritten thoughts. I didn't do it much in the beginning. It was all right for banter, but I wanted a record of anything serious that came up and took nearly everything Anita said about heaven seriously.

I asked what Anita's Father did with his time. "Studies a lot. We have permanently healthy teeth. There's no dental work or doctoring here. Daddy was disappointed at first but quickly found other interests. Streets don't need paving, sidewalks don't need fixing, and pipes never break. There are no manual laborers or manual labor; but Norman, *we* can E-mail telepathically to our hearts' content."

Until we were married, to my knowledge no Ober had a dentist in the family. Abe Rosenblum simply added me to the other family members he treated free. It bothered me. Anita said he'd be outraged if I tried to pay. When I needed a partial bridge, he ordered and paid for the denture. I asked Anita to go to his office and find the bill. It was eighty dollars. Imagine that today. I gave him a check. He tore it up. I gave him cash. He refused it. I said, "You can treat me for nothing but you can't go out of pocket for me." He didn't tear up the cash, just said, "Go to hell." After that he charged all relatives his costs, saying, "If my son, (he never called me son-in-law) pays, everybody does."

Returning to Anita: "Everyone here is beautiful and in perfect health. Lots are eligible here, but if we love living mates who still love us, romance never suggests itself. People with bad marriages in life find loving partners here. Others marry here when living mates take new husbands or wives. Not me. You are all I want."

"Life on the planets is for learning. It's not to be cut short unless it's physically unendurable. Most post-suicides leave us quickly to try life again."

Anita addressed lightly something I wondered about - why, if heaven's so fabulous, anyone ever reincarnates. "It can be the pull of living family. Still, as much as I love Timothy, if I can't be his Mammaw again, I don't want to be his child."

For a few months, when our first Colorado grandprodigy began talking, he called Anita Mammaw and me Mampaw. All too soon we became Grammaw and Grampaw. Anita was unhappy when Timothy stopped saying Mammaw. Now we're both waiting for Timothy's son to say his first words. Great grampaw would be nice. (He said it in 2005.)

Anita dealt with another subject I broached several times: "No, I *don't* know how much time you have left on Earth. All kinds of events lead to natural, accidental, sudden or intentional death, but no one living has a preset time to die."

"The death penalty is never imposed here. Felons, muggers, murderers and drug dealers are reeducated for honorable, peaceful next lives; but who's to say whether they'll stay that way or revert? How can evil not influence the living when governments are corrupt, when business and governments conspire to control power and wealth? How is progress possible when religions tailor God's aims to advance their own?"

That was the tip of an iceberg. Anita reintroduced the subject in later letters, indicting evolution and environment, too, as major impediments to

116

God's programs for strengthening love and elevating the worlds through human betterment.

Next Anita channeled, "I've signed up to study the universe's humanities (she learned later that she should have said universes) "and how much alike we are in spite of our different cultures "We know the Earth has no monopoly on human beings. I often meet people from other worlds."

"Men and women from two different planets fall in love here and agree to return together to one of their planets, which will be an entirely new experience for one partner. Linking destinies here, they expect their relationship to flourish wherever they go."

Three days later: "Your Sister Doris has left us to begin a new life. She, of course, knew where she was going, but we don't. We guess she chose the Boston area (where she lived two months past her twenty-first birthday)."

More on the peopled planets: "In class, we've discussed seven populated worlds. One student claims an eighth and ninth are out there, too, self-created." Later Anita learned better. "He was wrong. There were ten, none not created by God.

"Despite differences in conditions on each of them, our one God created life wherever it exists. Religious diehards – a poor word for the departed devout – see their faith in Him verified when they come here. Some call Him God, Christ, Allah, Brahma, Elohim, Adonai, Ahura Mazda and any of hundreds of other people or things worshipped through the ages. When we arrive here, we know for sure He's one God by any name.

"If I say Jehovah or Yahweh and someone else calls Him Jesus, Buddha, Divine Principal or Whoever, after awhile few here see Him as anyone but God."

In another letter: "You still itch for us to communicate verbally." That ambition seized me when Myron McClellan, a Denver mystic, told me it took him ten years to begin hearing the voices of the departed. Anita added, "I'm waiting to take a course on the subject. I hope it has an early vacancy. It's one I want to attend, not take at home. "

Hoping Anita could make it happen, I steadily inveighed over our channel for us to talk voice to voice. Myron McClellan told me to ask my Teachers & Guides for help, saying that everyone has them. Contact with them involves breathing exercises, recital of three psalms a day, patience, meditation and belief in God's infinite power.

The effort frustrated me for years of cajoling and carping at my Teachers & Guides, but hearing zilch from them. Tibetans, certain sects in India and naturals dispersed throughout the world are supposed to be good at this. I felt like I was retarded.

Reading, practice and expletives haven't taught me meditation. I eventually quit pestering my Teachers & Guides, but still recite the 23rd, 91st and 121st psalms, each once a day and do breathing exercises Myron taught me.

Anita continues urging me to keep trying and to strengthen my belief in God. "There are many accomplished lay spiritualists, eager for human betterment. Find one to work with you and one day you'll stumble past what blocks you." Eventually I did.

Anita expressed pleasure with my pace of learning to use the computer. She hadn't run into any in heaven. "Wise ones here trance or meditate to compute."

Another night: "Nobody here believes in Satan. Living people blame him as a way of putting their own bad behavior at arm's length. Demonic literature educates and appeals to Satanists seeking to dignify their sadistic tendencies."

And another: "There are celestial records here of our past lives. Anyone can access his or hers." Anita thought that reading past life summaries was supposed to help people not to repeat past mistakes. Convinced that our loving lives coincided more than once, she decided to wait for us to see our files together. I look forward to it.

At a subsequent bedtime: "There's no sun or moon here. The Light is a constant presence. But we see galaxies in heaven's sky. People on all planets name their stars and planets, but their astronomies are more like than unlike Earth's."

Another letter: "In one class, a man said people on Earth, like hackers invading computers, mess up other people's heads. The instructor said, 'Only in your head.'"

I asked her exactly how the worst characters on their planets became exemplary citizens in heaven. She offered, "For good persons, being in heaven validates lives lived decently and honestly. The bad are so relieved not being punished, they're angelic here."

It made sense to me that bad characters facing the Power that brought them from death to heaven are afraid to step out of line. But Anita thought, "With nothing to steal, no hunger pressure and only good treatment, they get hooked like everyone else. Nobody reincarnates intending to be a thief or killer. Even though our personal chemistries are purified, new malice and negative drives can arise from environment. Life is a harsh testing ground. Bad living conditions and greed can warp people into repeated evil lives.

"The Earth needs more opportunity, but there's less - more love, yet personal and national rivalries are as bad as ever - more and better food, yet there's no equitable distribution of something so critical to survival.

"I'm glad you want us to stay on here." I floated the idea several times. "I don't want us back in that cauldron of hate, hurt, spite, cheapness of life and disease. We'll stay here forever, just being ourselves, only better."

"Heaven's main jobs are receiving the dead and retooling their minds until they decide they're ready to live again. God can't force people or countries to do right. If He could, would there be wars? We're meant to improve - failing in one life, to try again. So far, planets' environments can undo good achieved here. But," Anita insisted, "Here everyone is reconditioned and ready for perfect mental and physical health. What we work at now is to make that state permanent every lifetime."

Next Anita took on a question I had asked seriously: "The sperm race is fixed, the winner's predetermined. The system's nearly perfect. Uncommonly the wrong one makes it by somatic accident. Also-ran sperm cells are retrieved to try again."

Then Anita sprang this one: "With incarnation and reincarnation so controlled, how come people are born crippled, or into poverty, brutality and in nations at war? Maybe the unlucky ones lived awful past lives. Maybe life on *planets* is their hell." She never did get us an answer to that one.

Anita provided interesting insights into her recreational reading. "I can borrow library books in any language in Mr. Kincaide's library, where boxes translate any text into English."

She mentioned Kincaide in earlier letters as kind and helpful and later as the man she relied on to direct her to information on the peopled planets. "We don't have Earth's current best sellers but we can study any world history and get the truth from scholars here who track and update the progress of all civilizations."

Most of her references to books in paradise have been drawn together here, starting with her answer to my question, "Do people write new books there?"

"Of course. Authors, editors, publishers, printers alight here along with everyone else. We have presses and printers ink for all sorts of books created here."

Anita channeled further, "Good reading is accessed either by visiting the library or by telepathy. Our bodies are light but our minds aren't. Heaven's full of good readers."

Anita was an avid reader. For some years, she was the librarian of the Robert Louis Stevenson School for emotionally challenged teen-agers. She mothered and steered them to role models in literature to help them confront their personal problems.

122

Anita's sheltered life ended long before her older Stevenson students tried to shock her with the obscenities of the day. She'd heard them all on U. S. Navy bases and from her prime source, her brilliant Brother Robert. Innovative off-color words and phrases as a fine art appealed to his erudite sense of humor. One of his classic letters from Fort Dix reported the number of times and in how many different parts of speech he heard the word fuck used in one twenty minute period. As intended, it cracked us up.

After the war I had two hernia operations at Shouldice Hospital in Thornhill, Ontario. Anita was with me for the first. She died before I had the second. During my recuperation from the latter, I read "Norman Corwin's Letters" (Barricade Books) to help keep my mind off my post-operative pain. In a letter channeled during my second recovery, I asked Anita if she could read along with me or ahead of me.

"I follow snatches and some whole letters depending on how carefully you read. I can't open a closed book or read ahead of you. Remember, I don't get the words off the page. They bounce to me off your noggin."

Anita went to a library that was new to her with our late close friend Jack Soskin who posthumously became my father-in-law (details below). A voracious bookworm, Jack was interested in everything ever published. His avocation was buying and reading whatever in print couldn't outrun him. He devoured pages faster than I skim them.

Professionally, Jack Soskin was an expert in antique rugs. His reputation took him to the White House, to exotic lands where sought after rugs were hand made and to museums, government buildings and appraisal sites of private collections. Jack and Sylvia Soskin were near and dear to us in New York City and White Meadow Lake.

Anita reported from heaven, "Jack still ferrets out odd subjects, reads them and fondles rare volumes to see how they're bound. He studies titles and credits, marvels at the many ways nascent civilizations invented to print and bind books. Block printed, hard bound, in light hands, they don't deteriorate, as treasures shouldn't. Automatic translation gives Jack, like any of us, whatever language we want to read in."

"We don't have to *go* to a library. I can order up reading matter for scanning at home or get on a waiting list for my turn to pick up real books that translate for me."

"The word propaganda isn't used here. Books with fanciful tales of the planets, like partisan historical reports, are in a section called ENTERTAIN-MENT. The fact that titles in constant use by our readers don't wear out is just one more miracle."

A miracle of my own kept me from wearing out from grief. After a surprising hesitant courtship, prodded by Anita, I proposed marriage to Benita Sachs, nee Soskin. Her Father (Jack Soskin) died of multiple myeloma six months after Anita's death. I met his daughter Benita during Jack's last illness and was properly avuncular in the beginning - there's a twenty-two year difference in our ages. Benita was fifteen years old when we first met Jack and Sylvia in the 1950s.

Benita was devastated by Jack's death. My interest in her had an unlooked for outcome. Two months after Jack's death I began having to remind myself that, though I appreciated her joie de vivre and warm heart, I was never going to marry again.

I wrote Anita, "I'm writhing in guilt over Benita. You promise you'll take my soul when my time comes and still bless me whenever we channel. You found God for me and convinced me there's life after death. I will treasure and love you always."

Anita: "I love you for what you feel for me and still make me feel for you. I'll always be part of you. Marry Benita and be happy." I still couldn't.

Later: "You've grieved too long. There's nothing wrong with finding love again." Remarkably, Anita and Benita tolerated my love for each of them. I proposed.

We decided I'd sell my house and she her condo, buy a larger house and get married. Anita applauded., "I want you to be happy. Enjoy life. You deserve each other."

Benita and I were married March 13, 1998 in Ellicott City, Maryland.

My first wedding was on April 14, 1943 in the Rosenblums' living room. Anita, a breathtaking symphony in blue in her trim light blue suit and matching pill box hat with a few inches of netting masking the terror in her eyes, put two small, icy hands into mine. I felt how frightened she was; but, before our families, we vowed to love and honor each other 'til death do us part.' Who thought then that, when death did, Anita would be the one to die and I'd find it impossible to accept the unacceptable?

A word to anyone who loved a lost mate so much that he (she) felt it would be disloyal to the memory of his (her) late spouse to think of marrying again. True, I had the advantage of a caring communicator who insisted I marry again. Well, you have me, if you want. I'd like to quote the mystic, Myron McClellan, who listened to my last bleats about my guilt over marrying Benita and laughed. "You, he said, "have the best of both worlds. Appreciate it."

Our late loved ones are happy where they are. They want their living partners to be happy, too. A New York cardiac specialist told me after Anita died, "Statistically, widowers don't live long after their wives die. Take my advice and marry again. You'll live longer. I didn't take his advice then but don't wait for good luck as I did. Find it.

PART FOUR

After Anita died, I drove our White Meadow Lake Hungarian friend, Nelia Feleky, to Florida every October and flew down in April to drive her back, staying a week, catching up with friends and family and scribbling Anita's channeled letters on yellow lined pads.

Nelia was in a small minority of close friends who believed in my letters from heaven. She asked if Anita could get her a message from her late Husband Leslie, an accomplished musician, composer and conductor in life.

I relayed her request and read Anita's response aloud to Neila: "I went where musicians like to hang out. No Leslie. Asking around, I was directed to a man named Julius who said Leslie was studying. Julius promised to tell him to contact me."

Nelia gasped when I read Julius's name. She said Julius Schwartz was a violinist who worked with him when Leslie arranged, directed and played piano for performances at Chez Vito, an erstwhile upscale Manhattan restaurant offering music and operatic songs with dinner. "But Norman," Nelia said, "Julius is **still alive**!"

Nelia immediately telephoned Hungarian friends and learned that Julius had indeed passed away. We were both eager for the next night's letter, which would be the last one channeled before I flew back to New Jersey.

Anita wrote, "I saw Leslie. His friend Julius *was* one of the violinists at Chez Vito. Leslie said to tell Nelia his feelings are what they were when he and Nelia met again in England (Their WWII reunion in London as Hungarian war refugees).

Nelia and her ballet troupe performed in England and toured the country until VE Day. Leslie told Anita he was convinced that being ex-patriots in England saved Nelia and her troupe from the Nazis. "For his part," Anita added, "though he wishes they'd had more years together, he's grateful for those they did. The war taught him to be patient. He says he will be patient until Nelia joins him in heaven.

"He writes and arranges music for concerts given here. I'm going and taking lots of family. He has composed new music here that he thinks will please Nelia.

"He's amused at your suggestions that she eat vegetables and salads. He remembers her Mother Ilona trying to make her eat them in Nelia's teens. As with all Hungarian ladies, it was command by understatement," unquestionably Leslie's words.

Back from Florida and decidedly depressed, I received a rewarding welcome from Anita. "I feel your emptiness. It happens whenever you're home from running away."

She enjoyed what she called our adventure with Nelia and my being jarred by Julius Schwartz's name until she learned that he *had* died. Anita accused, "You were sure you made him up yourself." I denied even a nano-second of doubt.

Leslie Feleky first became a distinguished composer, arranger and pianist in Europe. Later he gained modest fame in the United States. Anita wrote that she loved seeing Leslie play and conduct. "He spends most of his time composing and rehearsing. He says, tell Nelia he will be complete again only when she's with him.

"Leslie's music is well received here. He says that, if Nelia lives to be very old, he'll have composed more music here than on Earth, also that they have loved each other in earlier lives. In one, her name was Rose. And since no flower, only quartz (carnelian or cornelian) names Cornelia (Nelia), he often thinks of her now as Rose - because nothing about her is like quartz. Isn't that sweet?"

During another pen-written note at bedtime in West Palm Beach when I delivered Nelia Feleky there in October, Anita reproached me: "I don't like it when you jump on my lines with what you suppose I'm going to say!."

I protested, "When you're slow, I do sometimes jump the gun. I know I should wait. But what if nothing comes?"

Anita replied, "Then nothing comes. Try me later. Anyhow, I'm seldom that long. What follows the word darling has to be me, not you. It will be impossible to convince anyone our letters are real if *you're* not convinced." I asked if I ever did it and she let it go. She wrote emphatically, "Not on your life!"

About a year after this was channeled, Nelia and Leslie were reunited in heaven.

Two good friends of ours in the New York area - I'll call them Mary and Bill - had their bout with cancer a few years after Anita died. Anita wrote me one night that Mary was now safe from her ordeal. I phoned her husband Bill to offer sympathy. Nonplussed and audibly annoyed, he said Mary was asleep in the next room.

Upset, I asked Anita, who wrote, "***She's mortally ill. Her soul rests in her light body when the pain is unbearable.*** Mary's giving Bill time to survive losing her."

Mary alive, her soul in a light body in heaven? That was a solar plexus jolt to my belief system. Rereading the letter, I asked Anita, "Am I wrong or were you?"

She confirmed that Mary was now in heaven to stay. "God's remedy for unendurable pain is coma. Her soul went back and forth as she endured her agony until she thought Bill could make it. When she was in coma, her soul was in her light body."

On February 8, 2002, editing this book (again), I took to my computer to find out what heaven thought about capital punishment on Earth. She replied, "Evil doesn't exist here. Its extent on the planets is deplorable. But all else failing, God's is the best reform school. He doesn't punish, but once they're here, deceased killers kill no more.

"There's no guarantee they won't be as bad in their next lives, but their crimes stop and they leave with purified genes. God doesn't smite the wicked any more. We all come to heaven when life ends. During life we're on our own, good or bad."

Anita defined good and bad for her daughters who adopted their own definitions. She tried to persuade the girls and me to live up to the legend etched over the proscenium of the Ethical Culture Society's auditorium stage: "The Place Where Men Meet to Seek the Highest Is Holy Ground." It made sense to me and I know it worked for our girls.

More on evil: "When punishment by God changed nothing permanently, He began searching for an environment-immune magic bullet. His scientists, chemists and geneticists work on the problem, but immutably ethical civilizations have yet to exist."

The next day she fretted, "One suddenly trusting country or place would be everyone else's prey. People who don't lock their doors and windows are robbed and worse now. Any place with high ethical standards would be meat for the unscrupulous."

Later: "When God punished evil, His plagues and famines eradicated whole societies for the guilt of a few. Now He shuns retaliatory destruction as evil to end evil. Motivating humankind to embrace total equality is elusive.

"Failed reform efforts make things worse. Planets' histories are full of leaders more corrupt and bloodthirsty than those they replace."

Anita quoted a recent lecture she attended. "Krakatoa was God's last planned disaster on Earth. Unproductive, it sacrificed innocents and guilty. Ending planetary corruption that way would destroy all peopled planets, not just Enistor. God won't do it."

When O.J. Simpson was all over the Earth media, Anita wrote that the courtroom drama didn't excite Earth followers. "We all know the victims are better off here, though we oppose violence. Admission to heaven is on a no-fault basis. Guilt ending with death won't sit well with eye-for-an-eye mentalities, but evil didn't start in heaven.

"When punishment failed, He decided that evil had its base in His design flaws and that heaven must solve the problem with adjustments developed here. That's from our classroom lectures, in case you're skeptical."

"Each country's expunged histories anoint winners of wars as humanists, heroes and gods. Captains of religions, societies and industries pay writers to deify them. Bibles aren't true histories, they're creative, plagiarized and frequently updated legends."

Anita left Receiving to work with human betterment groups. Her letters were full of tidbits on her new job. "Some groups urge demonstrations of God's might to get people's attention. There are quick-fix plans for smiting away the problem, some ingenuous, some silly, most in between. Disillusionment here with massive revivals led by Billy Graham imitators were downgraded when 'religious' money raisers lost favor."

My solution was, if God won't punish the wicked, He might be persuaded to prevent them from doing business by removing chronic criminals alive and starting them over again. Anita thought it might fly - or maybe to humor me, she passed it along.

She returned to the subject soon after. "I tried your idea on one of the core group. His name is John. No, J-o-n. He mentioned it to a colleague who thought something like it was tried and dropped. Jon asked me to see if there's a file on it.

"He asks you to visualize how it might work. It can't be like in the movie 'Ghost,' when fuzzy, scary, gravelly voiced shadows hauled away dead bad guys' souls. Your idea is, grab them *before* they die, to stop their killing. Right?"

I adlibbed preemptive strikes to remove professional evildoers, starting them over knowing if they're evil again, they'll be removed again. "Incurable criminals get life in jail. Why not *remove* them? When people realize what's happening, it'll deter others."

Anita agreed that starting them over rehabilitated wasn't the same as smiting them fatally. "I'll tell Jon that. Keep thinking about it."

Anita's next news: "An enthusiast named Morton, who dislikes being called Mort, thinks *you* should be sent for now - not as an evildoer, but to help develop the plan here. Others say removing and restarting people will look like killing. They agree suddenly disappeared evildoers would deter others and criminals would get the message.

"They say your ideas are welcome and *you'll* be when it's your time. In heaven that's not long. You see a butterfly's life as short; we view the human span the same way. Waiting for you is easier on me than your waiting is for you."

Later: "Your bad guys idea has reached the core committee. They circularized other groups for reactions. Responses are coming in and you're not exactly being hailed. But old timers can't document that God ever turned it down and neither can I.

"The committee's interested. Those in favor are working on a detailed presentation. With no record of its being shot down before, it may fly. If anything is found, they're reluctant to prod Him. Your fans are those who want to do *something.*"

"Criminal-napping has been referred to a panel for further workup. I'm told its chances are slim because it will look like killing. See what else you can dream up."

That sounded like a prelude to thumbs-down, but I liked thinking my idea might squeeze through. The subject wasn't closed. Anita wrote further, "You're gaining ground, I think, because there's nothing better on the table."

"The more they discuss it, the more ways come up for making it work. Devoted thinkers from the planets and from heaven itself are debating it seriously."

"The panel worries that removal violates human rights, but it's clear that victims have the right to protection. Grabbing and reeducating criminals may look like capital punishment, but the greatest good for the greatest number has to be considered, too.

"Our thinkers say it would be nearly impossible to pluck every professional criminal from all societies. But they think it won't be necessary. Taking away prominent large-scale operators would make it plain soon enough that His power is behind it, so there's agreement that the plan merits a trial on one planet."

More: "Angels among people could designate candidates for 'withdrawal.' Pickup teams can be formulated. The safest way to deliver them here and how to store their bodies during rehabilitation are being discussed by a logistical team, just in case.

"Discussants favor not sending criminals back to life too soon, but returning them straightened out at their present ages. The hope is that God will find that more acceptable than terminating them. Don't look for anything in a hurry, but things are moving."

Anita was excited. "Groups here devoted to improving the universes know what an awesome job it is - but once you believe it's possible, you can't walk away from it."

Once in my married life I started to walk away from Anita. Six months after WWII, we were still sleeping in the Rosenblums' living room with no job in sight. Twenty dollars a week

139

from the government ("the WWII 52/20 Club") was all I had coming in. Abe and Lily, off for

a vacation, left cash to get us through their absence.

Demoralized, I packed a bag, intending to move to my Brother Ralph's home in

Brooklyn until I found work. Anita's irises dilated. I couldn't go. At the door I dropped the bag

and sobbed, "I can't." Days later, a small check arrived for a short story I sent to "The Bird

Dog Gazette," may it rest in peace. Not illustrious but a beginning!

Over a month passed with no word on my scheme for busting bad guys alive. Meantime, Anita visualized a new utopia for humanity. "If there were only haves, only prime real estate, good jobs for everyone and capital to finance high pay and full employment, centuries of evil would end."

I asked, "Can a group blueprint something like that that the wealthy won't oppose? The fun of having closed neighborhoods is keeping us riffraff out."

The mills of paradise ground slowly. It was four more months, Earth time, before Anita reported that God didn't buy the package. "He judged that, before enough criminals were removed for people to believe God was doing it, innocent people could be harmed." (Come to think of it, when Judge Crater and Jimmy Hoffa disappeared, nobody thought God did it.)."The core group liked the plan. They asked me to tell you to try again."

I don't see myself showing up in heaven and changing worlds. But Anita and I decided she'd continue her group work and when my decrepit carcass is cremated, we'd work together permanently – or at least until human betterment is up and running.

Turning away from tilting with evil, I must tell you how one of my most loved and respected mentors on Earth, Hector Chevigny, prodded heaven's betterment groups with an activist campaign to put some pronto into their planning.

This remarkable author was a feisty descendent of Canadian French frontiersmen. In his youth he was a butcher's assistant, hospital orderly, self-described backslud graduate of Jesuit Gonzaga University. ("My best course was girl pursuit.") Taught to "write radio" by boarding house pals, he became a broadcast writer at KOMO, Seattle.

His ambition to save up for medical school ended when Hector married Claire Graves, a boarding house friend who prepared him for his KOMO interview.

The Chevignys began raising a family on $35 a week and moved to Los Angeles, where he rose from rookie KNX staff writer to author of distinguished books on Alaska, meantime grinding out dialogues for Bob Burns's radio show, "The Arkansas Traveler," later the daytime radio serials, "Portia Faces Life" and "The Second Mrs. Burton." He also wrote what I think is his best book, "My Eyes Have a Cold Nose."

When we met, Hector was 100% blind and seemed to be 200% adjusted to it. I first saw Hector after joining WCBS Radio in 1947. My lowly job was covered by a Radio

142

Writers Guild contract and I went to a Board Meeting to meet real writers. Hector was on the

board, soon to be union president, and seemed to see everybody. I had a lot to tell Anita about

the scraggly bearded man with a Seeing Eye dog (Wizard) at his feet.

I kept quiet until a vote was taken, then raised my hand and was told that only board

members could vote. Asking which of them represented radio staff writers created confusion

until Hector said, "Nobody, that's who." Next election, one board seat was reserved for staff

writers and I was the first to fill it. Our beautiful friendship lasted until 1965 when he died.

The story of his heroic, contentious and remarkable career is one-ninth of my regrettably

unpublished book titled, "Nine Lives."

I want to tell you about his afterlife efforts to prod the process in paradise, not about his extraordinary life achievements. I caught up with him when Anita channeled in her August 13, 1995 letter, "Hector Chevigny's been here all along! He's sighted, beardless and a dashing *young* man. Claire's with him. He says they're enjoying youth a while before taking on being babies and asked me how the old coot is, meaning you.

They're talking about going back. He plans to grow up fast and write again. He says it will be a real kick getting around without a seeing-eye dog."

Wouldn't you think, after that news, I'd have had another letter about Hector in a few days? The next casual mention was on February 23, 1996, over five months later.

Then this, on February 28, 1996: "I told Hector about your latest books ("Tata" and "Nicodemus"). He quipped, 'Have him send them up to me. I'll set 'em to rights.' He and Claire are like honeymooners."

The next mention of our ex-blind friend was on June 28, 1996 - which brings me to the point I want to make. I carped for years with Anita about it always being now in heaven. Letters about Hector, spaced apart as they are, graphically illustrate how time *doesn't* pass in heaven. While the months roll by here, as indicated by the dates of the letters, there is no tomorrow in heaven as Anita drummed into my head all along.

Continuing the June 28th letter: "Hector has no beard. His skin is clear. He's handsome and elegant, like a courtly southerner – but he's still Mr. Mischief from Montana, especially when he breaks into Western jargon." (One result of his working on the Bob Burns show was his habit of slipping into Bob Burns's Arkansas drawl whenever the mood hit him.)

"When you come, he promises new stories about the Flathead Indian Yeshiva." There was nothing religious about Hector's gamey tales of the alleged activities of a Montana tribe of Jewish Indians with a wild, unbeatable football team.

Almost five months later: "Hector makes the most of being sighted. He always has something beautiful to describe. There's plenty of beauty to go around in this scenic playpen. He digests it whole and describes it beautifully in Arkansas dialect."

144

"I introduced Hector to Bill Ober, who complained to him, 'The surfeit of good fellowship here is my only burden.' That made them instant friends. Hector says Bill has more pizzazz than Puck, is a 'tetch' weird but brilliant."

When I asked how she met Hector in heaven, Anita wrote, "I was doing my group thing and he walked in. I didn't recognize him the way he looks now until he mentioned his name. I told him mine – he never *saw* me in life. He'd heard about the groups and came in to check us out. Imagine - Hector! If I were alive, I'd have dropped dead!

"I told him about the human betterment program. He knows the universes and how God's work is attacked by evolution and environment. Hector said he'd prod God into asserting His full powers, claiming, 'He's sufferin' from burnout, needs a pep talk."

Anita introduced him to what she called bigger guns – "Philip and Kortin, two of our more thoughtful types. They enjoyed him and swept him off for a tour. They were gone quite a while. Several times during their rounds people came and asked me if I really knew Hector in life and was he like *that* then?"

The answer is yes. The building his apartment was in is on Gramercy Park. It had one hesitant Otis elevator, with shiny brass work seldom seen any more and a sturdy rope you yanked down for the elevator to rise and up for it to descend. Hector maintained that, when tugged, the rope woke up apprentice writers who ran on a treadmill to make the elevator move. Anita and I never tired of Hector's Canuck-Montana-Arkansas blarney.

145

When he got back to Anita, he said he'd learned a lot, stirred up the troops and reckoned he'd get in it with us. He promptly shook up the group bigwigs, calling them holy goldbricks without the gumption to get going.

Anita tried to mimic his dialect, "'Y'll never git offa the dime without'n I git a fahr lit under the lotta ya.' Hector wants to have a quiet talk with 'The Old Man.' Heaven hasn't gentled him much. He loves Bill Ober. The two belong in the same cage."

Anita reported more Hectorisms in later letters: "He sniffs around human betterment operations, buttonholes anyone, asks questions and makes suggestions, looking for areas to improve. He says we all have to get out on the fahring line, among the people, face down the rascals, get them out of power and win back the worlds."

"He's made friends with an activist group who want to carry big sticks. People who have been down that road are wary. They say God will turn rough tactics down for reasons they've all heard before. Hector is hotter than ever to talk to 'the Head Honcho.'"

Then: "Your Hector will drive us all to reincarnate. I knew he was strong minded and persistent, but I never knew how much of each."

Early in 1998: "Hector was at a Universal Human Betterment meeting – that's what we're calling ourselves these days – and told the central committee that he and you working together could clean up in a few weeks what's holding human betterment back. He fell into his drawl and allowed as how his pardner (you) will make big changes in the pace of things soon as you young down again.

"He lathers his irreverence with humor, so even opponents enjoy him, I think. They wouldn't get too exercised anyway when he cuts up. Will you discipline him or will he turn you into a backslud Jesuit?"(Good question.) Anita added, "Hector knows he's Peck's bad boy, but says it's in a good cause. He calls the pace here boondoggling and thinks God should attend committee meetings – he says he's overdue for a pep rally with 'The Top Banana.'"

Springtime: "Hector tackled committee records and isolated seven duplications I missed. Claire is pitching in to help him. Did I say she's beautiful? Nothing like how we remember her! Hector wisecracked about her assistance, recalling his blind days. 'Back then, she was my more or less resented amanuensis.'

"He's become the librarian of the human betterment groups. We're eliminating old fashioned cross-referencing and putting everything into easily tracked files. I appreciate it because I went through a lot of history trying to get a handle on my job. He snorts at the old files and describes colleagues as do-gooders with no notion of how to do good. Nobody takes open offense, but he's starting to scare everybody."

Shortly after, "Hector keeps heckling long timers, calls them marking-timers – some have been at it that long – with no intention of wrapping it up. That brought on a meeting of the central group to explore his charge. There's no blackballing here. They're stuck with him and, they pointed out, he with them. Hector pushes as far as he can.

"He told them anyone who didn't get results this long in New York would be fired. He was gently reminded that he's not in New York. One of the elders mentioned that he might be happier in New York. That's as far as anyone has gone to tell him off.

"Hector allowed politely that human betterment has been kicked under the rug by every organized society and would never come out from under it if left to well-intentioned amateurs. He pleads for more aggressive ideas and action. He brought you up again, saying if he had his druthers you'd be sent for now. No laughs. He said the job needed more idea guys who respected deadlines – apprentice writers would do it faster."

Later this: "Your friend Hector Chevigny is turning out to be more trouble than your Uncle Harry."

Further: "Hector's treatment is heavy with politesse. He's getting no-where – *yet*, he says. What troubles me (and me) is, he keeps promising them real action when *you* arrive, and causing hooded glances at me. I worry about Hector's plans for you."

Then this: "Some of his victims sigh when he appears. One suggested that his energies are consonant with the goals of reincarnation. He threatens them regularly and they're concerned that the two of you will behave like floggers on a Nile barge."

The last entry on Hector: "He was asked politely to find another interest and allow the process, as it's called, to proceed at its own pace. He'd become testier, which is not good form here. In the time he's been inveighing, he made no converts and, he told me, is just as happy to apply his energies elsewhere. He saw the end coming, took it well and put the best possible face on it. Around your New Year's he and Claire reincarnated."

Anita's reverence for God spreads throughout her letters. The subject is too big to consolidate in a single batch. I won't try. What follows describes her first sight of God:

"Were Mother, Daddy and I **thrilled!** Norman, *we've been in God's presence!* He's not in recognizable form. We saw an oval clouded aura surrounding a strong light about twelve feet in diameter - maybe more. No heat comes from His Light. He didn't exactly overwhelm us, but His spectacular appearance was supercharged with love.

"He never spoke. He stopped, turned one way or another from time to time. I mean, His aura turned one way or another. Mother and I were together. As He approached, Daddy skidded alongside us. Nothing was said by anyone.

"Light bodies tried to move with Him, to keep Him in sight until they had to stop because thousands of others were waiting. I swear He stopped and looked at me - with neither eyes nor face, creating a powerful sensation that He was looking right at me. It wasn't intimidating; it was inspiring. The upper part of His aura seemed to nod my way.

"Mother and I took root. I whispered to her, 'I think He was looking at me.'

"You know Mother's twinkle. She said, 'or me.'

"I can't describe what raced through my mind in His presence. You as Pragmatic Pete would have said nobody could be sure what was inside the aura, but you wouldn't now. I've been in God's presence, Norman, and He defines heaven."

Anita went on, "Nobody bowed, knelt or cried out. As far as I could see, people just stood in awe, their eyes fixed on the moving oval passing above us. When He was out of sight, an afterglow lingered. Until it faded, nobody spoke. I understand now why religious practice is superfluous in heaven. When you've been in His presence, you have all you could pray for. Beauty, love and selflessness are embodied in Him."

I've seen Anita affected by great dramas or musical extravaganzas, powerful books or persons whose interests touched her. The sight of her daughters left her breathless at special times. The wooded paths at West Point Farms exhilarated her. Her love of beautiful people and places overcame her shyness and unlocked her capacity for joy. But nothing she ever saw or did in life affected her like the sight of God in heaven.

PART FIVE

As you've been reading, reincarnation attaches itself to almost any topic about heaven, which made it impossible to tie that subject into one neat bundle. The collected references that follow provide part of the picture.

"We have an efficient system here for receiving souls in the afterlife and, when they're ready, starting them in new lives. It's the biggest 'industry' here."

"While here, we live in true serenity. Some settle in for a few of your years and then, challenged or restless, opt for the action, struggle and opportunity to improve their next lives. But once back in life, their intentions are too often distorted by problems. Hard times retard eagerness to reincarnate, but the system here *somehow* subtly encourages it or we'd have a terrible glut of generations reluctant to leave."

"Sooner or later virtually everybody reincarnates, but in the womb or once life begins, we acquire our future by touching other lives and being influenced by them. Destiny is definitely not ordained but accumulated."

"A life ends, another begins. In recycling, *no soul is wasted.* We live in temporary bodies in splendidly surreal surroundings, made whole from last life traumas. Then reincarnation starts with the chemistries of one man and one woman united.

"When contraceptives interfere, *unutilized life-giving materials reclaimed from spent sexual fluids and ovulation are re-used for future pregnancies.* Eventually, under God's benevolent management, almost all souls are candidates for new lives."

"Some young people are so adventurous here. They talk to persons from other planets. On impulse, they hop off into new lives on one of them – for a lark, it seems. I marvel at their courage and caprice.

"The feeling here is, big deal, if my next life doesn't work out I'll come back and try again. Euphoria of anticipated opportunity boils over, leading modest numbers of us to make quixotic or quirky decisions, exiting heaven like kids on a toboggan slide."

"Did I mention that the combined number of humans and animals continually recycling is pretty much finite? All souls regroup in heaven. Unless you hold back – like Mother did – you advance through the same vault of light again and again."

"It's easier being Jewish in heaven." *Anita's Achilles' heel, the Holocaust, unsettled her post-WWII years. Anita could see no movie or play, read no book about it, wept when the subject came up. Her heart broke for the millions whose lives were snuffed out. She could never lay them to rest.*

"There are many impediments to reincarnation: wars, the economy, jobs disappearing by the thousands – these don't spur the spirit when life here is so appealing and *safe.* We know death isn't the end and that we're in a safe haven of love, warmth and caring. Once back in life, conscious memory of heaven is lost.

But that doesn't stop reincarnation when, pressured by environment, too few succeed in bettering their lives."

"After a lifetime in or near New York, where there's so much pre-occupation with self, this divine retreat is utterly enchanting. It's no disgrace to delay reincarnating; prolonged periods between lives are neither applauded nor stigmatized."

I asked Anita more than once why anyone would ever *want* to leave paradise for an uncertain life and she answered patiently, "Because we *know* that, if the next life doesn't go well, heaven will take us back. That certainty and a compelling silent force here stimulate the brave and eventually the hesitant to go for the brass ring again."

Later: "I've said reincarnation erases conscious memory of past lives. But memories of all our lives remain with us in what (Carl Gustav) Jung called the collective unconscious, as good a name for it as any."

Anita's conscious memory invariably trumped mine. In any argument she could recite every nuance of my alleged derelictions, some before we met. I could never remember hers. Enjoying her memory edge on me, she won our skirmishes in a walk.

She didn't think Jung had it exactly right. As she pointed out: "A lifelong smoker reincarnates with no addiction. But if his mother smokes during pregnancy, addiction can be reintroduced. If the mother doesn't smoke and the father does, breathing in his smoke, she can habituate her child in the womb. Or

155

the habit's regained when a newborn begins breathing its parents' smoke. Is that collective unconscious or collective bad judgment?

"Take a household full of hate, violence, political extremism, fanatic opposition to women's rights and other sick addictions. Negative home influences infect or re-infect offspring from birth, if not before. Does the collective unconscious never forget?"

One more time: "I've seen too many reincarnate not to believe that, although going back seems a decision by individual choice, *something* subtle stimulates it. God must have discovered early that nobody would leave heaven if reincarnation weren't engraved in us. We *must* be programmed to live again. You and I will be on a short list of dedicated freaks if we stick to our resolve to remain here for eternity."

Another time she wrote that couples might disagree over reincarnating. "A husband may declare he's going back. His wife may not want to for reasons of her own. Usually, not always, they break up and go - or stay - their separate ways."

This came during one of my depressions, aggravated by heavy snow that shut me in for days: Anita asked, "Still have your doubts about heaven, don't you?"

I fudged the question. "Reading my mind again? I have *moments* of doubt – just moments, not like I was. I get seizures of desperation when it crosses my mind that, if I'm kidding myself about our letters, I'll never see you again - that these letters may be in my head because I can't accept the thought of being separated forever."

Anita said, "Believe me! Meantime, I'm better off here and I *know* what I know."

Later I questioned the obliteration of conscious memory of former lives. "Wouldn't it be better for people to *remember* and use memories of past lives to grow?"

She answered, "The very first generation of reincarnates had an awful time. They returned to life with all their memories. Many in their second lifetimes, remembering their first, made chaotic attempts to reunite with surviving first life mates and families.

"Men, who were killed or died young reincarnated, grew up and hunted down their past life surviving spouses, older and remarried. Former and present husbands fought and died over them. That problem disappeared when conscious memory of past lives was ended."

Our topic pendulum often took radical swings. For instance I sounded off, "I'm dying – I take *that* back – to explore our recorded past lives and see when and how we shared them. I *know* we did. I wasn't smart enough to fall in love with you as fast as I did. Past lives together must have turned me on to love you at first sight."

Anita answered, "It may be true, but we might discover that I had to reform you every lifetime. Hindus believe they keep going back until they conquer bad karma and win the permanent reward of Nirvana. I think Nirvana's right here, right now."

I responded, "Without sex? Nirvana must be heaven plus sex."

Anita replied, "Earthy sex, my brooding rooster, may spark reincarnation for your ilk. If you're over-amorous here, you won't be long deserting me."

Then she worried, "Living here indefinitely, dedicated to ongoing programs, is a sacrifice. Few volunteers in permanent residence here don't have family ties or friends still living. Giving up reincarnation means abandoning sex as it's known in life. Only our aboriginals don't have that problem. Everything they are they always were. There are no female aboriginals. The men are happy living here and working for God. They sometimes quietly resent humans, but it's not because of sex."

"Not having peeked at my past lives, I have no evidence yet that we shared any of them. But it's a given here that true lovers' loves renew from life to life. You and I might have been brother and sister or, who knows, adulterous neighbors once or twice."

I decided, "Nah. I'd have tied a knot around you whether you married me or not before I'd make you be illicit."

Anita one-upped me. "Constancy to me probably resulted from profligacy in your earlier existences and disgust with your immorality." She taunted further, " I may have reformed you after you died of a social disease."

I clicked back, "According to Doc Lindwall I was a rabbi, pure of thought, deed and without the brains to defend myself." End of debate.

Anita, on another night: "If a strong hand guided all destinies always, nobody would be born to abusers, die in childbirth or get AIDS. That strengthens the argument that control here is limited. If everyone lived under His eye, we'd all be Cinderella, marry handsome princes or rich girls and live happily ever after. There are too many people to keep track of. The living *must* be responsible for their destinies."

"Reincarnation can be risky. Newborns get new identities *if* they survive abortion, stillbirth and birth accidents. Next come risks of crib or other premature death. The road of life has unexpected detours; but I know prayer absolutely does help."

Change of subject: "Norman, cemeteries aren't places of repose. Souls aren't in graves. Cemeteries are for-profit real estate for disposal of spent bodies. Heaven is where our souls repose, for eternity or less, as we ultimately choose."

Anita had a caveat. "From what I see, eternity starts idyllically but the feeling doesn't last forever. It's never another lover, fighting or disagreeing - love doesn't wear out here, but desire to remain can ebb for no *apparent* reason. Few people choose afterlife eternally. Repeated life cycles are natural to the species.

"Being here eternally – more for some than others – eventually dulls the pleasure of pasturing. Parting with your mate can lead to a new relationship in paradise; but just as often, the remaining mate thinks it over and reincarnates later.

"Will *our* resolves hold? Do you have the stomach for prolonged failure? Will no fast breakthrough in human betterment thin your determination? It did Hector Chevigny's. I love it here. I'll love it more when we're together; but if you decide to reincarnate, I'm going with you." Couldn't you just be crazy about her?

I said, "Sharing parts of a hundred lifetimes can't be as good as eternity together."

Anita wasn't finished: "Eternity started before there were people on planets. God created the aboriginals first to help Him work out the universes, planets and habitation. They neither age nor incarnate. For them there's only eternity in heaven, but for us, there's choice and I choose to act with you."

"I'm nuts about acting, but always develop goose pimples before a performance," says Anita Rosenblum of the Senior Play cast. "I'll probably become a dental hygienist, which, although a comedown from acting, will afford opportunity to be dramatic — if only over sick bicuspids." (That came from Anita's "celebrity" interview, which was in the 135th Annex Supplement, Wadleigh High School OWL, April 28th, 1936.) Their yearbook was loaded with classmates' autographs and, alongside her stunning graduation picture, her brother's comment: "The ugliest one in the book." Little Robert struck again!

"Nobody begins to count God's miraculous powers. His existence isn't argued here. He's held in awe. We love Him. Living humans have doubts. Here in His domain, we *know* God is real. We know, too, God *doesn't need us to pray to Him when we're not asking for help.* But words of love and concerned prayers for others can't hurt."

I asked, "Do you have a picture of God? Have you seen him with His clouds off?"

"Nobody has *seen* Him. There are artists' concepts of what He looks like. We guess at why He isn't visible – some say that, since He existed long before the peopled planets, He's so ancient and frail that He doesn't want to be seen that way.

"I doubt that. All people here are young. I'm sure He is, too. We're healthy youths-for-the-duration. His presence in His cocoon may be so awesome that clear sight of Him is overpowering."

"God's major miracles are his construction projects; building and spacing stars and planets, inhabited and not, and meeting gigantic logistical and materiel challenges."

"Another of God's miracles is light bodies congregating in any number without crowding. Heaven's spaces adjust to hold a few or a multitude. A lecture comfy for a dozen is just as comfy for thousands. I've asked how that happens and don't understand the answer, which is 'higher dimensions.' At my brain level - I like to think it's improving - I try to confine my questions to answers I can grasp."

"I'm more attached to my immediate past life than most here; because of you, I guess. We aren't the only twin-flames, but after a while, few past relationships on the planets rival the bliss of sharing God's country; and though most stays here are limited, many transients enjoy the pleasures of paradise longer periods before leaving it."

Anita's home life hadn't been paradise, but deeply attached to her family, Navy life in Oregon made her homesick. Letters and phone calls weren't enough for her. In seven months there before sea duty, as I completed advanced sea duty training, rated an Aerographer's Mate 3C, Anita, by herself, ran a kindergarten on the naval base.

The only time she wasn't homesick was when her Brother Robbie, changed from round little boy to a tall, lean beanstalk, spent a lively month with us, hiking, picnicking, joining trips down the Columbia River to Pacific beaches and working at a fishery in Astoria, full of humor about his smelly work and coworkers. During his stay, deferring to his sensitivities, no grilled Chinook salmon, pride of the Columbia River, was prepared.

Like Sampson, Tongue Point, Oregon was a glorious gift, though we disagreed at the time about God's hand in our being there.

In one letter, Anita reflected on how age at death affects heaven's young. "The ônes who die young usually reincarnate at the median age here, seeking full next lives to make up for what they missed." Not my Brother Harold, he liked heaven best once she was there. "It's unusual that your Sister Doris had two shortened lives." She had told me in one of our letters that Doris was back in heaven not long after her reincarnation, a victim of crib death – no longer an Ober.

"Daddy thinks about reincarnating. He says he gets embarrassed watching others leave. Mother and Daddy say it's a lot like friends dying on Earth. Mother's contented here. In the end Daddy will stay where she is. But as family members and friends re-incarnate here, being left behind again makes him think."

"People usually try to begin new lives connected to living family. Since they can't be born again to the same mother (assuming they wanted to), another is found, often in the family. Reincarnates start out as well-aimed chemistry, but there's no guarantee."

Anita doubted that many reincarnate for juicy steaks. "That habit has to wait for the second teeth. If they could skip childhood and go right to steak, meat eaters might leave faster, but what rational spirit gives up the joys of heaven to be born to a screaming woman, mother's milk, mush and years of domination for hamburgers?"

"Reincarnates' next lives are skewed by environment. We're programmed to recognize the mates we want to remarry; no loving couple chooses a future destined to part them. But there's less control as families move apart for so many reasons these days. The remarkable thing is that so many continue to find each other."

There's assuredly a lot more to know about reincarnation – but that more or less ended Anita's comments on the subject, fascinating for believers and, I suppose, fantasy for atheists and fiction to subscribers of religions that teach denial of its existence.

The next night, she talked about memories of immediate past lives. "Seven and a half years after my life ended, it takes determined visualization to retain my memories. Few of us here, absent communication with the living, continue to cherish past life minutia long. Staying in heaven when friends and family reincarnate, many remarry here, make men or lady friends or become reclusive, forgetting because they prefer to.

"Paradise is balm for those whose living mates forget them. We neither pine nor wither, but flourish in ready new friendships. Selfless, undemanding loving relationships often make the afterlife more pleasurable than life was.

"Commonest practice is naturally man to woman, woman to man. Gays and Lesbians are neither favored nor opposed. Nobody reproduces here. Homosexual unions, like all others, aren't furtive or overpoweringly physical."

Anita had reported that nobody is born with a fixed number of years and days per lifetime. But forever afterlife with her is a siren song to me, which amuses her. "Since you've gotten religion, you like the idea of eternity underwritten by God. But if I know you, when you get here, you'll ask for a written contract to stay as long as you like."

166

My war "contract" lasted almost three years at Uncle Sam's pleasure. Anita was able to terminate hers with the Navy in Oregon with the arrival of my sea orders. Anita had to spend carefully at Sampson. Her Tongue Point teacher's pay ended our dependency on rescue checks from her parents and helped us afford trips in an ancient Hudson every other weekend to Portland, the Cascades and Pacific beaches split by the Columbia River. We'd have seen more of the Oregon Grape State if the old car weren't waiting for new parts so often. Alongside Highway 30 near the naval base, we picked big succulent blackberries. Anita filled quarts of jam for us and to ship to our families.

At Sampson we paid Uncle Sam $11 a month rent, 70 cents a month for electricity and 40 cents a month for water. In Oregon, rent and utilities were free to Anita as schoolteacher. Her cherubs and their mothers adored her. When my sea orders arrived, mothers begged her to stay on at Tongue Point for the duration. But we followed my orders to San Pedro together, determined not to separate until my ship sailed out of sight.

Before Anita died, my daughters Dody and Amy never had trouble buying me birthday presents. Anita knew what I needed and tipped them off. After her death, facing the challenge without her, my girls have done remarkably well, considering that I never know when clothes are worn out or discard a pair of socks before they're holier than thine. Later Benita took on the responsibility of defending me from my sartorial lacunae.

The girls picked up where Anita left off, making it their job to recruit me to a spiritual life. One of their inspired cooperative gifts was a weekend at the Omega Institute in Rhinebeck, New York, a fortress of New Age learning in lush wooded hills overlooking the Hudson River Valley, two hours by road north of New York City.

Omega gave me an unexpectedly fascinating weekend. Students of all ages shared eclectic to eccentric views of cult and occult religions, alternative paths to wellness and bodybuilding, also exotic cultural and inspirational events. My classes illuminated for me just how far Anita had brought me from atheism since her death. She kept an eye on me there. On my first night at Omega she couldn't wait for us to talk about the place.

"Shamanism, found among early Buddhists and discovered by Marco Polo, eventually hopped out of Siberia, embraced by Eskimos and Western American Indians. You can be comfortable with Shamanic divination that what grows thinks. A tree, a shrub, *all* nature has its own awareness. Living things support each other while, among people today, there's ever less farmland to plough and ever more destruction of open acreage to create housing, malls and industry."

I enjoyed my courses, fortified by Omega's hearty natural meals, bright, enthusiastic students and its lovely lake with wooded walking paths in every direction.

Guided by Tom Cowan, I remember vividly my first encounter with Shamanic beliefs and practices. His lecture on working with nature set the stage for a phenomenal communion with Anita I'd like to share with you now.

Our class took part in what became for me an extraordinary outdoor experience. As instructed, each of us selected an individual tree in a hilly wooded area near our cabin schoolroom. We sat with backs to tree trunks, facing in turn north, east, south and west under a bright blue sky delicately etched by fast moving white clouds.

We were at each position several minutes, holding pads and pens - writing down what, if anything, we observed facing in each direction. In my first position, as I hoped to make contact with "my" tree in some way, my eyes became riveted to a cloud among many moving overhead, shaped as an unmistakable sketch of Anita's head and face! The wind played with her upswept hairdo, the way she wore it at our wedding.

There were no eyes. There was no noticeable expression. But it was Anita's head and neck up there, moving with the wind. I scribbled down what I saw and caught up with the others who had already shifted tree trunk positions.

I immediately looked up. There was no sign of the Anita I had just seen. But there was *another* view of her with free flowing hair. Again she didn't smile, nod or take notice of me. But how she excited me, passing above; how she tore my heart open. Tears clouded my eyes, making writing difficult.

I scribbled away, struggling to regain composure, and couldn't wait to look up from my third position to see if Anita was *there*, too. She *was* – grander than her predecessors, crossing a large clear blue canvas, this time engaging my eyes with hers, at least with the outlines of two sockets etched in her milky white face.

I believe I cried her name, though I can't say for certain what I did. I had to be called by classmates to assume the fourth position. Again I stared aloft in hope and excitement. Anita *couldn't* be there again but there she **was**, less distinct, more diffuse than in her earlier portraits, dissipated by the wind or waning energy. Tears came without shame as I wrote about the fourth revelation high above me.

There was a young woman in our class named Anita. Back at the classroom, participants described what their tree spirits helped them visualize. Some reported no results, others ranged from wind whispered predictions of things to come, and directions for achieving requested boons or other heart held objectives.

When my turn came I was overwhelmed trying to speak. The young Anita of our group hugged me until I found words for the four portraits etched in the sky. In two days and nights at the Institute, only this event led to tears and exultation.

My Anita's comment in our next letter was, "I knew what you were saying but you couldn't know what I tried to say to you. Even outdoors, cumulative energy can be too full of stuff – other people's, or of the Earth, trees, bushes, rocks and pebbles."

I asked her if *she* had projected her images. She said that the episode arose from my love for her and nature's cooperation. I blessed her for inspiring the tree and me, even if *she* wasn't gliding by in the sky over Rhinebeck. If Anita didn't do it, God himself must have inspired what I saw. They were no mirages.

Anita's comment: "Omega initiated you into a culture that recognizes communication among all things in nature. It helped you accept how much is open to us in life. If the weekend did that for you, it was worth everything."

Another memorable event took place during a later trip to Denver to visit my Daughter Dody and her family. Dody had made an appointment for me to have a session with the mystic I mentioned earlier, Myron McClellan. Scoff if you want –I would have once - but he brought Anita's spirit into the room for a loving visit through Myron. I spoke aloud to her. Myron supplied her answers, which I couldn't hear from her.

In our letter that night, Anita was euphoric: "Wasn't that wonderful? Norman, I just know there's divine purpose in our letters. Maybe learning about us will open others to seek what we have found and to believe in God, the afterlife and reincarnation."

"God's ear can't personally hear every soul in every universe. Try to imagine how many people pray to Him at any one time – and in how many tongues! Not that prayer is wasted; it's an outlet for people in fear or torment. Messages for God register not from the mouth but from the soul. Heartfelt prayers process here, with the frivolous and flagrantly self-serving ignored. The rest go 'upstairs' for response.

"As with my cancer, not all problems yield to prayer. People pray to win the lottery, but the folly of gambling doesn't move God. God's miracles for the needy are formidable, but the Almighty is not omnipotent, no matter what the 'good' books say.

"People say 'Thank God' when they avoid accidents, get someplace on time, find something they mislaid, remember someone's birthday. God doesn't say Gesundheit to every red-nosed Norman who's God-blessed for sneezing."

Sneezing! I've mentioned Anita's younger brother, Robert Rosenblum several times. Now a multi-published professor of fine arts at New York University, an icon, critic and lecturer in the art world, he was born brilliant, with a far out sense of humor. He wasn't fifteen when we met. Too smart for me even then, his favorite line to his sister during my sneezing marathons of autumn was, "Neetery, you married a lemon!"

Anita channeled sporadically on one of her favorite subjects, animals. What follow are some of her comments on them in different letters:

"Some creatures were created toxic if eaten, because they were meant to share the land with man. But great carnivores exercised their taste for weaker species, including toxic ones, until even they were extinct, as man learned early to hunt and eat flesh.

"Big disappointment here attended the loss of the dinosaurs. They were intended to be vegetarians, domesticate, work and live in harmony with man as towering proof that humans could never be all-powerful.

"As he honed his intelligence, primitive man sharpened his craft to trap and use animals as food and for work. Maintaining herds replaced tracking them in the wild."

"No animals reincarnate at their volition. All but small birds, cats, dogs and horses recycle right after death. Animals in the human food chain recycle immediately until greed, droughts, environment and evolution make them extinct. "

The next night Anita added, "Domestic pets have more rights here than anywhere else. Horses aren't ridden and don't haul loads and as I said, they're not eaten. But none choose when and where they reincarnate."

I asked, "Are there pigs, chickens, sheep?"

Anita was patient. "Pigs, chickens and other food animals recycle when they die. Eventually, all pets return to life. That may disappoint animal rights advocates, but like it or not, animals are in the celestial plan for keeping people fed. Birds make habitats here until they're reincarnated, as other domestic animals do."

Anita, her mother and both of our daughters adored cats! Generations led good lives with the Rosenblums, with us and with our girls. Dody gave them up for parrots, which are as popular with her husband Les as cats were with me. Bumsy, Pushkin, Misty, Willoughby (one of Amy's), Millie, briefly Dody's – I can't remember the rest. They amalgamated as Nicodemus in children's stories I told and wrote - a cat who always outsmarted the hot-headed father. Dody and Amy grew up on tales of the wily cat and his servants. Later, Anita and my grown daughters used to eavesdrop when Nicodemus lived again at bedtimes for my Grandsons Timothy and Michael.

Anita's wooly but not wild contribution was the true story of Bumsy, a wayward mother cat who surprised the Rosenblums by adopting a wretched little baby kitten they rescued off their street. Bumsy carefully cleaned and fed the orphan only after doing the same for her own litter. Her talent for escaping the apartment for wanton liaisons kept the Rosenblums searching for homes for the kittens Bumsy brought home to hatch.

More on creatures in heaven: "Wild animals don't share paradise – neither do spiders, mosquitoes, houseflies, gnats, rats, mice, lice or bedbugs. Despite the Adam and Eve myth - or maybe *because* of the Adam and Eve myth - there are no snakes here."

175

Another bit about animals: "Creatures on some planets live centuries. I've seen illustrations of awesome carnivores and great vegetarians inhabiting unpopulated areas, seen when humans stray into their terrain. These beasts are described as capable of moving mountains. The only way to survive the flesh fanciers among them is escape."

"I meet newcomers who still worship animals, suns, clouds and rain. Seeing that no pig or goat runs this show, they quickly come to believe in God."

"We read about planets with only animals that reincarnate, but with no people. Among these myriad species, some reproduce without mates."

Back to humans: "God rejects occasional impatient suggestions from aboriginals to blow humans away and make something better or stop trying. He also won't turn planets into paradises until people turn their swords into ploughshares and learn to love."

"A prevailing concern here is that each new war inflicts greater destruction. No treaty lasts. When massive power is assembled, war soon begins. Successive holocausts wait only for countries to rearm, regroup and send their slain here.

"If they can't do better, it will go on until each peopled planet destroys itself and human life exists nowhere. So I do sometimes wonder why God *doesn't* just erase His flawed experiments and start over or declare that human life is an idea that failed.

"He may be waiting for the planets to self-destruct. When the last is depopulated, He may like the universes better without people. What will happen to humanity when the last holocaust ends life on the last planet?"

She fretted, "Some religions hold that heaven is already crammed – that, as they tell us these days, there's no reincarnation. He may let the last wave of humans scamper about paradise as we do now. But - should we grow restless and want to reincarnate, what happens then?   He is a patient God. Will He be patient forever? I don't know."

Anita wrote that nobody is ever ill in heaven. In one letter she made this comment on sickness on the inhabited planets: "From what I read, though names differ, similar diseases affect every peopled planet, from the common cold to cancer.

"On some planets, strains of influenza Earth has a handle on defy medical science. Only one planet has no respiratory diseases due to continual seeding of effective germicidal elements in its atmosphere. Average life spans vary from planet to planet."

In consolidating Anita's references to death I discovered that the subject usually requires respect for its context. This section will connect some observations on death that shed light without citing mentions better left where they are:

I was very moved when Anita channeled, "I'd come back to you undead if I could in good health, 75 going on 76 (as of that letter) and be your loving noodge (pain in the neck or anywhere) again. Wouldn't our friends and family be surprised if I turned up!

"In case you're wondering, a while back when you brayed at God, I inquired about returning to life. It's *almost* impossible. My physical body no longer exists. A soul permitted to occupy the body of some person near death seems the only way.

"I looked for official word that it's possible and, without ceremony, my name was added to a long list. I supposed that to mean that, if everybody ahead of me got living bodies or changed their minds, my turn might come. One thing they look at is *your* condition. They won't send me back to you if you're on your last legs, old feller. If your number was up and my number came up, I'd stay right here."

"Deaths that move you move me, but not to tears. I react to sad things. No *rule* says we can't cry, but we have no tear ducts and that's that."

"Was I better or worse off when I died? Better a hundred times, because death rescued me from cancer. Was I better or worse off the last months of my life? Worse, because I suffered from pain and foreboding! Swift death was what I prayed for. I wasn't sure and that frightened me for a week or so. After that, I knew what I wanted to happen.

Anita made me promise not to send her back to the hospital, no matter what. I never left her except to shop. Her final diet was a powerhouse of nutrients blended in a "malted" to keep her from starving. Anita had been a shy girl when it came to using the toilet. At such times in Sampson and Oregon, she actually shooed me out of the cottage.

I remember our snail's progress when she had to use the bathroom near the end and she had to depend on me. I held her waist, her hands on my shoulders – keeping her from falling as we shuffled from the bed to the bathroom. She called me when she was done and we shuffled back. It broke my heart watching her lose ground.

"Anticipation of death," she wrote, " is worse for unbelievers and people like me who want to believe but are confused by people like you. I wanted to believe in God and spirituality. You were sure we had nothing to look forward to."

She was right. I wrote, "If I thought there *was* a heaven to receive you, I'd have rejoiced. Not believing was torture."

She replied, "Now that you believe, don't fear death. When it's your time, don't hold back. Times and circumstances of death are the worlds' business. God's plan is for people to live full lives. For one thing, it helps slow heaven's intake from the planets."

"When you're here, you not only regain dearly beloved me but you lose your shaky heart (with stents in it), clogged arteries, arthritis, diabetes, eyeglasses, pacemaker, cataract corrections and repaired hernias." (*Robbie was right – what a lemon!*)

I asked, "I just have to wait?"

Her answer was, "We're taught here that every life's for learning or relearning. Never be so sorry for yourself that you shorten your chance to live, learn and improve."

"God created ten universes; one destroyed itself and He can destroy the rest. There must be a point when civilizations are so evil that He terminates them. There's so much hatred; so little meaningful help is provided to

180

those in need, there may come a time when humanity's wickedness leaves God no alternative."

That led Anita to reflect on past lives. Explaining why no birthday or anniversary is observed in heaven, she wrote, "Birth and death days are recorded in our past life histories. But can you imagine every one of us celebrating every birthday we ever had?"

More: "Accepting all who come here saves a lot of record searching, interrogation, finger wagging or whatever might otherwise apply to different levels of misdeeds attached to past lives. When the Lord decided that punishment achieved nothing, He freed heaven, too - from inquisitions and meting out penalties."

Two nights later we talked about past lives again. "It's taught here that past life experiences are encapsulated in our subconscious memories as instinctive guides. In and out of the womb, those memories exert somatic and psychic influences that shape our instincts, judgments and performances."

"Mother, Daddy and I are attending lectures on past lives. They dug into theirs, made notes and, between lectures, look up past life relatives. I'll disown any that you and I didn't share. I'm much more interested in learning about yours. I'd love for us to discover how you fell out with religion and how and in what life you were hurt as Doc Lindwall says and in which one and why you were murdered."

"For you, living into the next century is no longer far-fetched. (I reached that goal over five years ago at this writing.) Stick to your diet, keep taking long walks and visit me often on our private line. I'm not medicine but we are tons of tonic for each other."

This from me: "When we're together in heaven, I'd like to look into my past lives, too, to find out what I ever did to deserve you loving me."

I doubt if that displeased her but she wanted to talk about something else. "It's not uncommon for someone to be your parent one lifetime and the child of your child the next. It's best that the living don't consciously remember past lives and have to sort out who was what to whom and what we all were to each other earlier."

"Affluent people reincarnate faster than schnooks who struggled in their last lives. But affluent new life isn't guaranteed. You could be a tycoon one lifetime and a pauper the next, a raving beauty one life and a gargoyle the next. Today's Bowery bum may have been yesterlife's emperor of industry."

"A good life can be either accident of birth, genetics, hard work or all the above. We're born to love and help one another. But too often we fail to earn love. Once people truly love, they say here, they're ready for eternity in paradise."

"We won't be sure until we explore *our* past lives that we've taken twin paths more than once. But I *know* that what drew us together was within us, not in our stars."

"There's no hard and fast evidence of what survives in the subconscious and what doesn't. What we do learn in each life imprints in the subconscious and is carried from life to life. Absent damage from birth to death – a large IF - our smarts remain intact."

Anita approached the subject again. "Healthy minds and bodies are born of survival and growth lessons absorbed in past lives. Past damage carries along, too. Capacity to learn and grow in each lifetime is impacted by parentage and environment."

Anita liked telling this joke about a dialogue between a grandfather and grandson:

"Zaydi, vhat makes lightning?"

The old man scratched his beard. "God alone knows."

"Zaydi, from vhere comes vind?"

"Who knows? It blows."

"Zaydi, Am I boddering you vit my kvestions?"

"Never. How else vill you loin?"

She continued, "We should survive longer and our growth capabilities increase with each lifetime. If the worlds were perennially peaceful, not prize parcels being fought over, succeeding lives would be better than past lives every time.

"When the differences between God's plans and human actions end, people *will* live longer; there'll be no premature death. Birth and death won't hurt. There'll be no disease or stress. People will be well all their lives. Voluntary dates of death and rebirth will stabilize populations. Human warehouses will close as all of us *decide* when to die."

"Debate over the death penalty misses the point. Here where life begins, nobody is executed; but many societies give themselves 'legal' rights to substitute their judgments for God's. When a killer is killed, society is saying two wrongs make a right.

"Killers and killers of killers arrive here on equal terms as God's efforts continue to fortify societies with the will and ways to stop what drives humanity's inhumanity."

Our dear friend Barbara Apisson, last of our West Point Farms family in Central Valley, NY had just died of cancer. Anita said, "You're the last ones left – you, Dody and Amy - mourning the end of a lovely time and place in our lives - but death doesn't scar us as it does you. We care. Dody and Amy care. I'll look up Barbara."

Barbara Apisson's recipes are featured in "A Diet for 100 Healthy Happy Years, Prentice Hall, 1976, which I wrote from the notes of Dr. Morvyth McQueen Williams, a gifted and early outspoken alternative medical doctor.

"No one here mourns when one of us reincarnates. Though it means parting as surely as death does, we see it as the beginning of a new adventure in possibilities."

Anita reflected, "Life's beginning functions well enough. Death can be untidy. Ragged endings spoil too many lives. Why must there be heart attacks, strokes and lingering diseases like cancer? Life must end sometime - why not easily at a self-selected date and time? Can't intelligent craft and less moralizing let life end benevolently?"

A rabbi called Anita's Uncle Iz's (Iz Lipkin of Chapter Nineteen) quick death God's kiss, a nice way to describe the sudden, painless end of a good life. Anita said, "Every death should be blessed with God's kiss. Sloppy, painful dying shouldn't be a matter of luck. I think we need to form a group here to improve the *way* people die."

"The living have no visitation rights in heaven. Since you acquired faith late in life thanks to your angelic wife, spare yourself doubt. Go gently when you die. I have no premonition of your impending arrival, but when it comes, enjoy crossing. I will yours."

I chimed in, "That's exactly what I want. Even if our letters turn out to be delusions, believing you're in my future holds me together."

Anita wrote, "Live as long as you like it. If there's pain and no remedy, choose the easiest way while you can. The transition will set your soul aglow – and mine."

Anita, though enjoying her busy life after death, didn't miss much that went on with me. She said, "I skip some of your stuff by choice - don't linger for bowel movements or when you urinate. But I almost always respond to our channel. I can't activate us as you do me. You can whistle for me - I can't whistle for you."

185

I asked in one letter, "Do subconscious memories of heaven lead to suicides?"

She said, "I'm not in touch with my own subconscious, let alone anyone else's. I wanted to die to escape what I feared more than death. I have no reason to *think* my desire to die came from subconscious memories of heaven.

"Pain makes people beg for the balm of death. Some say pain before death is purgatory, that painless death comes when punishment is uncalled for. I think some are luckier in life and death than others and that the real luck of heaven is heaven."

"Whatever brings death, we're pain free from then on. If flawless pasts were required, the population of paradise would be zero. Everyone slips sometime, but most of us are decent humans around our lapses."

"A number of otherwise reasonable religions oppose suicide and try to impose their views wherever and whenever they can. Some of the same arbiters have waged wars, embraced the death penalty, oppose equal opportunity, suffer without pain large numbers of poor and yet are against suicides that poverty and desperation cause.

"God doesn't turn His back on anyone in enough pain to take his own life. People with the courage to end their lives, for whatever reason, *may be* evoking unconscious memories of God. Those memories may strengthen the attraction of death, because of the glorious new beginning death promises. When

186

religions accept past and future lives – most don't – fatally ill believers won't have to wear away from massive debility."

More about suicide: when I went into a deep depression, I wrote Anita, "I don't see a reason to live. Going your way has lots to recommend it. I'm lonesome for you. Would my committing suicide jeopardize our future?"

Her reply: "Norman, I want you with me as much as I wanted the Carlisle (my WWII ship) to sail back to the West Coast so we could have a few nights together. We argued a lot but I never wanted us apart. From when I gave you my heart, you became my existence. Don't end your life unless your body's attacked and defeated as mine was."

Anita said, driving home after the first fatal diagnosis at New Jersey's Dover General Hospital and a second reading at Hackensack General confirmed it - "I don't fear death. I fear cancer. They say nothing can be done for me. One thing can. The sooner I die, the sooner I'll be pain free. If you love me, don't let them keep me alive."

Back to our channel: "Nobody here greets suicides with horror. To me, the rest of your life is a disease separating us; but there must be purpose in it. I'll always love you, but live your full time." I cry when I think of her words.

Anita linked my living on to what she was convinced I had to do. She warned against "…distractions that interfere with your writing. I'm sure your destiny is to do something with these letters. You may be scoffed or barked at, but some will believe."

That subject came up again when Anita worried that it might be hard getting readers to accept this book as real. "If we're published, skeptics will say they're your delusions. I write the way I wrote my letters to you during the war years, but can we expect credibility with readers who don't know anything about us?"

I could say only, "Time will tell."

She wondered if she should study more; resist prattling and channeling love letters - just stick to heaven. "I'm too ready to chat − us being us fills me with pleasure."

I said, "Just keep them coming. Your letters sustain me. Anyway, I'm leaving out most of our goofy asides and small talk."

I asked her again if she knew when I'd be joining her. "I wish I could tell you or that your demise will be fast and painless. Neither is decided here. You and your environment determine that. I believe, when asked in prayer, God *can* help. But your time of death is in your body, not His hands."

I tried another approach: "Will I come to heaven knowing English, a pinch of Latin, French, German and pidgin Yiddish or do I forget them?"

Anita answered, "In time, we retain only what's useful to us. We know nothing we didn't know before until we learn it here and there's little you can't learn if you want to. People come and go. Scholars stay longer. They find heaven intellectually stimulating. Dumbbells usually reincarnate faster than smart ones."

"Life ends with death. True and false religions tell us what to think about this." Between life and death, she said, we're exposed to more craft and artifice than fact. For instance, when I asked her about UFOs, her comment was, "With only one inhabited planet in each universe, none able to communicate with another, where can UFOs possibly come from? *We* see them as man-made events, hush-hush experiments, military and private flights. Most alleged sightings and all kidnappings and tampered-with victims are creative, hallucinatory or both. Claimants trade their 'experiences' for money, attention and wish fulfillment. It's a living.

"Criminal elements are behind some UFOs. They transport drugs and other contraband, moving their operations around to escape arrest. Some of these unlawful activities eventually become IFOs. Secret military, industrial and criminal flying objects stay under wraps as long as their sponsors find secrecy advantageous."

There was a postscript the next night. "I tried UFOs out on Mr. Kincaide at the library. He always looks mildly reproachful when I bring up a subject that's not in his personal Dewey Decimal System. He found nothing to substantiate them.

"There's more boloney on UFOs in your libraries than here. We have nothing that talks about fakers, quacks and crackpots. What little there is treats UFO lore the same as reading palms, tea leaves and telling peoples' fortunes."

Anita's sense of humor was working when she used the phrase, "I enjoy putting my two cents in." She said, "It's meaningless here. We don't have two cents to put in. And there's no two cents plain (soda water), no nickel-a-shtickle (five cents a piece) or pennies to pay for your thoughts. No ten cents a dance – dancing's gratis here. No planet has been pelted with coins or bills from heaven - maybe from airplanes."

Anita brought irascible (I used to think alleged) ghosts into our correspondence this way: "Be grateful I'm not a poltergeist. If I were, I'd torment you good and proper."

I promptly asked, "You have poltergeists in heaven?"

She said, "Not here. YOU have them. Harmed, cheated or killed, too outraged to let go, their souls cling to the scenes of their traumas. We have none because, when they stop stewing over what irked them, they come here aware that their bad tempers and destructiveness were scary nuisances.

"Incredibly angry poltergeists need help surrendering their territories. Exorcists do their mumbo jumbo and take credit when the aggrieved soul vacates the premises. Volunteers from here name a few well-liked antecedents waiting for them in heaven. It's all it usually takes, but ornery ones need coaxing. A dug-in poltergeist can require drawn out negotiations, interrupted by quirky disturbances that alarm the living. Poltergeists can challenge our celestial teams, too, but not for long."

No celestial team helped Anita fight her cancer. One doctor scolded her for not seeing him sooner. Her rapid descent from a youthful, pretty seventy-year-old woman to hollow death surprised her doctors. It was predicted that she would die in six months. She died in six weeks.

PART SIX

Anita's notes on the peopled planets began bravely. "I'm in a storehouse of records. In this enormous place, thank God everything I pick up to read automatically translates into Earth English! The room I'm in is called Inhabited Worlds."

Somewhat later: "This project is **huge**! There are a gazillion files I haven't opened yet." Anita's mother and father were reading and making notes, too. "Without them I'll never finish. Planets' names in heaven aren't what they call themselves. Our world is identified here as Xonthus." We agreed to stick to names used in heaven – except Earth. It seemed unnatural for us to call it Xonthus.

She continued, "Ten planets had human life. It was dumb thinking we were the only living people. Nine of the ten have people now - striving, growing, living, aging and dying. Some have better lives than others, but no planet is perfect."

"No science fiction hordes are poised to destroy Earth or each other. Animal worlds have species unknown to us, surviving as on Earth - at one another's expense."

My reaction was, "Animal worlds? Will they be in your report?" She promised to investigate them but doubted that paw-print hieroglyphics would reveal their histories.

193

More: "The word *'universes'* better defines how populated planets are situated in their spaces. Each has its own sky and solar system. Contact among them is intentionally impossible, to keep one from contaminating or invading another."

More: "There *were* ten populations in ten universes, but the planet of one is no longer inhabited. All the peopled planets are numbered experiments. Two suffered cataclysmic catastrophes. On one, Enistor, depopulation is total and permanent."

"The ten universes were set up before *any planet was* peopled. Then planets were chosen for potential habitation, favorable climate, food, shelter and human growth. Living species were started on each planet one at a time. Human and inhuman creatures quickly discovered their appetites for worms and for one another.

"In the beginning, foods that supported one species poisoned others. It took many modifications to get each civilization off and crawling. Unending battles for survival were fought, with the strong killing or enslaving the weak. Today, peopled planets are not crime free and lack equitable sharing of wealth, food, climatic conditions, raw materials and humanity. God's universes are still works in progress, improvement needed."

That's how Anita described Dody, sometimes Amy and always me when she was particularly frustrated by her daughters' teen rebellions and the laissez-faire culprit she blamed *for not quelling them. I remember her exact words on one such occasion: "I soften you up to get them things they want badly and **you** come off smelling like a rose."*

Back to business: "The possibility of creating new atmospheres to accommodate new forms of life is under continuing study. Unpopulated planets can be tapped to repair major wasted areas in peopled ones, dropping in bedrock, replacing rich topsoil lost in dust bowls – all such calamities were anticipated, except atomic destruction - or Albert Einstein might have been called here before he completed his destructive formula.

"A lot of space debris results from natural explosions, novas, meteor collisions, shooting stars and the gases and muck civilizations throw into their atmospheres. They're drawn off from time to time but God's patience isn't endless. Today, miracles are withheld if man-made problems can be solved by man."

That brings us to Anita's notes on the peopled planets. I've relentlessly boiled down the series of long letters she channeled to me over a few months.

Anita began with the oldest peopled planet, identified as Experiment #1: "I read about secants, sectors, lineament, thrust and other things not defined, which I gather have to do with locating and fertilizing planets chosen to be peopled.

"Experiment #1 is coded 7274, whatever that means. Later planets have lower four digit numbers. It can't mean the first planet was peopled 7274 years after heaven opened its doors. I'm trying to find out what 7274 means in relation to heaven's eternal timelessness or whether we're even talking about years."

I asked who wrote the Enistore notes. She said, "Probably people who died on their one terrible day or victims who trickled here behind them. They don't say." She corrected my spelling. "It's Enistor, by the way – no final e."

I asked, "Did Enistor scientists discover atomic energy? *Did* God destroy them? Did they blow themselves away?"

Anita answered, "The file writers don't seem to know. I guessed an atomic explosion. The people of Kerak, one of Enistor's two continents, occupied the planet over seven thousand of their years. Earth from BC to AD was longer than that. So 7274 *can't* mean our years. Mr. Kincaide, the librarian, promised to find out what he can.

196

"Enistor's rotation isn't like Earth's, where light and darkness follow each other predictably. People lived in permanent sunlight and wild animals in perpetual darkness. Exploration of the dark lands proved fatal, so it stopped.

"Civilization caught on slowly. It was centuries before speech developed, then a form of writing and hand-written pamphlets by and for small numbers who could read them. There were no books or newspapers. Elders taught the young, orally, I suppose. Enistor never achieved what later planets did, because of endless wars and never-ending coups, invasions and theft of anything or anyone they could carry away as booty.

"On Enistor as on Earth through most of its history, women were chattels, serving men and bearing offspring. Being caught preferring your own sex meant death. At its highest level they never attained what Earth people had by 1000 BC. There were no large cities. Everything was hand crafted or loomed. They developed animal husbandry for food, skins and wool. Some animals worked and lived with people.

"Enistorans were ignorant, sluggish, lacked reasoning and imagination. There was no social ferment. Communities were clusters of crop farms near water. Trade for food, clothes and other necessities was by barter. To live well you needed something to trade.

"Enistor has two large continents, Kerak to the north and Duniak to the south, separated by oceans. Many small islands lie off their coasts. Some off Kerak were used to isolate 'trouble-makers' from 'normal' society.

197

"Vague religions existed on both continents, but efforts to preach about a god earned adherents segregation or death. A form of emasculation was adopted to prevent new births among believers and stamp out worship. Believers took refuge on some of the islands before Enistor came to its end.

"Kerak's average life span grew to something like fifty years, Duniak's forty-seven. Their year, based on the planet's rotation, seems to have been roughly 280 days, about 200 with more daylight than night. Enistor's seasons were spring and fall, no winter or summer.

"No hospitals are mentioned. People who got sick either recovered at home or died. The sick took to floor mats and waited. Causes and cures were mysteries to the end. Members of families saw to one another, though fearing illness.

Proposing change meant exile or death. Men had great strength but had no recognizable social structure. The two basic industries were the food supply and building sheds and shelters. Taxes were levied on animals and food farms but rulers gave nothing in return. There's no word on how rulers got that way, nothing about elections.

Settlements formed loose unions for protection, but disaffected groups changed alliances, often bloodily. "Homes - shacks really, had no plumbing. Water was carried in leaky wooden pails or, in greater quantities, by ox-like animals pulling wheeled water wagons, deliberately tracked over crops to make use of water leaking from them."

"Few on Enistor were educated. The self-educated were generally swept away by the strong men and their minions. Enistor, which every community called something else, doesn't offer much material for study."

I asked what they wore. "Skins and woolens. If cotton was grown, they didn't manufacture, barter or name anything that sounds like it. Trade was unreliable. Ships were crude and sailors feared the oceans."

"What did they eat?"

"What they could. They knew spoiled food kills but not how to recognize or retard spoilage. Their best effort was blocks of ice chopped from frozen lakes and ponds that border on the sunless regions, hauled to icehouses, using sawdust to retard melting."

I asked, "Did they have paper and ink?"

"Bark sheets, papyrus-like paper, inscribed with natural dyes, scripted in inbred dialects. Few people wrote, fewer read. Writers died without teaching successors, who learned to speak and write differently. But suddenly everything stopped. Enistor's souls came here confused with no idea what wiped them off their planet."

Reviewing what Anita gave me on Enistor, I saw nothing on religion except that leaders rejected gods. I asked her about it while I was editing these pages. "The approved 'religion' was enforced ruler worship, no religion by any standard. Leaders killed to seize power and were killed in turn. Their 'religion' was a device to police the population."

Anita didn't believe they took it seriously, but fear of death, as some of Earth's churches discovered, resulted in manageable worshippers. No more on Enistor.

The next night Anita turned to Thetas, Experiment #2 "It has the number 7102 which, if I understand it at all, means it began 7,102,000 some-things ago. It's not another Enistor. First, it's still peopled; second, it has a deist religion, an official temple preaching one God and a theology that promotes goodness and mercy.

"Their one God is worshiped throughout the single vast land mass, which I guess is as big as Eurasia with North and South America tucked onto it. No inland seas or large lakes break up the continent, just a huge ocean surrounding one great lump of land.

"Scattered offshore islands are sanctioned havens for outcasts. Mainland cities are far apart. Populous centers share trade, business and organizational plans. There's no federal capital like Washington, D.C. and there are no sky-scrapers, though some tall buildings could probably be put up using marble-hard plastic blocks invented in Thetas.

"There's no monetary system. They have more processed than natural food. Everybody works and is entitled to free provisions, a subsidized home and the right to reproduce. Time borrowing (explained below) applies to workingwomen who have babies or anyone who has an accident or illness interfering with work.

"Licenses are awarded for conception of babies. All generations of a family live together, usually with a grandmother and grandfather caring for children while their parents work. Two children is the legal maximum, as it is on most peopled planets.

Two was the number Anita and I planned – no accidents, no mistakes, to borrow from one of Anita's favorite anecdotes. As a little girl she asked her father if she was an accident, He answered, "You weren't an accident - you were a mistake."

More on Thetas: "Few families have more than two babies because time borrowing kicks in when a woman takes leave to have a baby. Pay doesn't stop, but to keep unpaid make-good time low, mothers spend only brief periods with new offspring, rush back and work overtime until 'owed' hours are made up. Recovered sick workers and accident victims pay, too, through uncompensated overtime.

"Workers get early retirement to keep younger families employed. The important jobs are in trade, manufacturing and food. With no money there are no banks, just bargain and swap - goods for goods, services for services, or goods for services. Each city meets its own needs and regulates trade in surpluses, balancing demand and supply.

"A six day work week prevails during daylight hours. Part of the day of rest is for church. The only night work is make-good overtime. Nights are free time for people with no newborns, accidents or sickness to atone for.

202

"Day and night are about equal. Two rotating suns service the northern and southern hemispheres separately, each of which faces its sun's rays and darkness in turn.

"People are short. Five feet is tall for men. Women are an inch to two taller, making for a different relationship between the sexes. Men revere their women. When not reproducing, women do the hard labor. Men run businesses, govern and teach. Schools train young boys and girls to fill society's needs."

I wondered if God made women taller in Experiment #2 because they got a raw deal on Enistor. Anita thought that subtler sexual inequality prevailed on Thetas, too. Short men respected their taller, harder working wives, she felt, because marital discord was bad for war, business and sex. "But there's no sacred feminine ideal," she said.

She continued, "There's no leisure and nearly no crime on Thetas. Children, after first year half-days, attend school all day long. Nobody under sixteen is allowed out at night. It doesn't say sixteen what. Radio and television provide only information.

"Dinner-to-bedtime diversions are movies and live entertainment but no nightclubs, shooting galleries, pool halls (prostitution and drugs aren't mentioned). Everyone but overtime workers goes to bed early.

"There are typewriters of sorts, no computers. Electronic devices are coming. The binary system's been figured out and efforts to build computers are under way.

"What else? Rules forbid premarital sex. Copulation follows what they call binding, which means forever. Divorce is unheard of. Churches don't marry couples. Civil offices 'bind.' The fact that it's for life doesn't discourage Thetans. Marriage is the way of life."

Anita and I were married April 14, 1943 in the Rosenblum living room. An otherwise pleasant rabbi, seeing my navy dress blues, bemoaned hasty wartime unions. That living room became our bedroom for almost three years after WWII. Benita and I were "bound" by a municipal court clerk March 13, 1998 in Ellicott City, Maryland.

The next night I asked about travel on Thetas and learned there were no railroads, trucks or buses. They use boats, barges and ocean steamers that hug the coasts and riverboats that carry mainly business traffic. Coal, oil and natural gas aren't mentioned.

"Caravans of animal drawn wagons carry goods overland from city to city and bring raw materials and other products back. Cities have paved roads and sidewalks. Bicycles carry people to and from work. There's little pleasure biking, except for young people sneaking out on church days to break the rules against pre-marital copulation."

I wanted to know what the people looked like and Anita said, "More or less like us. They have smaller skulls. You can't say smaller brains; their business acumen outstrips most of the Earth's big thinkers.

"There's no love of music or art, no cultural pursuit. Couples seem to bind for someone to talk to. There's no humor, no comedy, no practical joking.

Thetans are a serious society. Its people spin like cogs in perpetual motion wheels."

"No notes describe what anyone looks like. People are like robots. Copulation's their big recreation, topping films and live shows. Thetans are sexual animals. A common language is taught as part of business training. People who can't make it in business are trained for service or food-related jobs. Water is boiled to pressurized steam for power. That's familiar."

Another letter: "Homes get electric lighting and heat when it's needed – which is rarely. Household tasks are performed by hand. There seem to be no kitchen gadgets.

"Climate is mild due to the two suns. There's little rain and no snow or blizzards are mentioned. Apparently inexhaustible springs feed their rivers. Pipes carry heated steam to workplaces. Like every necessity, water is free."

I opined, "Business may like Thetas, but does anyone have fun there?"

Her answer was, "Thetans might think we're clowns with our prurience, cheating, divorces and drug culture. They have no vices – not even tobacco or alcohol."

The details were sketchy. When I pointed it out, Anita said her source material was sketchy. We left Thetas there.

After some small talk, Anita pushed on: "Experiment #3, Grania, has the number 7002, which I'm still waiting to have explained. Granians, to their credit, believe in both creation and evolution - that God made and evolution changes their world.

"They have two seasons, very mild, rainy summers and coldish drizzly winters. A huge sun permanently over their equator – they call it middlebelt - keeps densely soaked air masses circulating north and south constantly. The tropical latitude, which they call pohoth, is unpopulated across its unbearably hot, soggy width. As the planet rotates, all parts of it catch heavy rains continually soaking habitable areas."

Heavy rain recalls a very soggy memory: after my discharge from the Navy, before we took the train home from California, Anita wanted to check out the fabled Bullock's department store in downtown Los Angeles. (Macy's absorbed it in 1996.) A sudden downpour caught us on the wrong side of the street, overtaxed the sewers and flooded the busy streets in minutes. Anita's umbrella was too small to share. By the time we got to Bullock's, I was soaked. My shoes were waterlogged. Anita fared better. I stood inside the door shedding a pool while she flounced off to shop, giggling. My wretched state from the downpour made her laugh for the whole trip back East.

Back to Grania: "Permafrost caps both polar regions, Ora (North) and Sora (South). Nobody lives in either, but they're explored for minerals and raw materials.

She said there's no dominant continent. A dozen Australia-sized independent states rise from their wide oceans, living peacefully as socialistic societies. Treaties regulate production and distribution – states grow or make non-competing products suited to their climates and resources. Some export foods, others raw materials or manufactured products.

"Gold, silver, platinum and diamonds were discovered near the perimeters of the pohoth. Their industries use all four but the torrid belt is too dangerous for mining operations. Instead, inventors have compressed glass into diamonds and other ingredients into platinum, gold, silver and baser metals.

"Students from every island compete to study at educational campuses. The successful stay on to work and live. Good scholars become teachers. Scientists, technicians, artists and artisans learn at schools that teach every craft and skill, providing talent that increases output. The young are encouraged to specialize and many do.

"Universities groom students for governance. They graduate to pools and await jobs created by death or retirement. Commonly, single or married students leave their homes for school and never return. The state sees achievement as a minor god.

"Strong governing bodies enforce strict codes of ethics. By law, parents choose children's mates in the cradle. Refusing to marry a contracted mate is illegal."

Anita continued. "The states regulate music, drama, movies, television and radio - and just about everything else. There's one political party – tough-minded Realists.

"Retirement is mandatory at sixty-whatever." Equivalent numbers kept her guessing. "Government pays workers and executives for their entire careers. Medical care is state supported. Diseases are thought to originate in the pohoth and to travel to populated latitudes in soggy air masses. The situation is under study but immunization is something they haven't stumbled on.

"There's heavy use of gas and oil for cars, trucks and heating, but heating is a minor item in most areas. Manufacturing complexes have perfected screening methods to eliminate polluting particulates and neutralize poisonous gases. Workers produce in five 'day' increments and government controls commerce in all products.

"A husband, wife, boy and girl make up a family. Sexes are pre-determined. Injections after birth insure an exact ratio of males to females. People multiply at approved times after marriage. Marital and educational schedules are compulsory.

"There's less sex on Grania than in other worlds. It's seen as necessary, but it's not particularly popular. Craving it openly between impregnations is a sign of bad taste.

"They have no crime, no social or physical abuse and no competition. Housing is standardized. At state stores, everything goes with the job. Every able person works. Pay continues during illness. They allow four 'months' off after childbirth, after which child centers take over. Parents share homes with children until the young are employed.

"Nobody's buried. Cremation is handled by the state. Death isn't mourned. There's a short respect period, but lasting mourning is discouraged."

Anita's footnote: "Grania works, up to a point. But I prefer life on Earth for love, emotion, caring and excitement. A lot that we don't like about our lives doesn't exist on Grania. I doubt if they're better off for it."

Speaking of love, emotion, caring and excitement on Earth recalls this WWII comedy of hope, stress, frustration and reward. The USS Carlisle was in an eastbound convoy from Hawaii headed for San Francisco when our orders were suddenly changed at sea. The problem was - five of our wives were driving north together from Los Angeles to meet their husbands when our ship changed course from San Francisco to San Diego.

None of us was friendly with a ship's radioman, so no covert message could go to the ship ahead in the convoy, which was continuing to San Francisco. But the signalman in our quintet flagged a semaphore appeal to a signalman he knew on that ship, who promised to phone our hotel there to tell his wife to go back to San Diego.

That base covered, we couldn't wait to reach Dago. Sprinting to a pay phone on the pier, I called the hotel to turn the girls around if they didn't get the word and meet us in a San Diego hotel. Then I phoned the state police, explaining our crisis, to ask if they could head the ladies off en route. I told them the color of the car, its plate number and described the women. Then we took off for the hotel to get rooms and wait for our wives.

Amused but sympathetic, the state police were on the lookout from San Luis Obispo to San Francisco, but the girls had left earlier than we thought and got all the way there without being spotted. Appalled, worn out, then hysterical with laughter, the girls jumped back in the car and headed south. The police alert and description of the car with five navy wives was broadcast up and down the coast. The story was in the next day's papers – with no results. But we lost only one day of their company.

Anita and I couldn't imagine that happening on Grania. In fact, with no pleasure in sex, we agreed, Grania will never attract the tourist trade.

Our longest letter, mercifully shortened here, describes Experiment #4. It began, "Morcot is coded 6989. I'm still after Mr. Kincaide for help with the code." The help Anita got is explained later in Chapter 46. We came close to understanding it, I think.

Morcot's population occupies an area about the size of Colorado in an otherwise small barren planet. Morcot's peopled plateau, though elevated, lies below a ring of mountain peaks towering over it. Its population of well over three million is dense for the limited habitable space on the plateau and its slopes. The weather is bitter most of the year. In the mountains, without shelter or shielding, survival is impossible.

"In the hot season," Anita wrote, "daytime is up to thirty-six 'hours' for something like three 'months'; huge melts flood the plateau and turn frozen tundra into lakes, ponds and reservoirs. Returning winter brings back hard freezes and sometimes strict water rationing.

"Year round waterfalls supply energy and enough ice is melted to ward off water famines. In shortages, electricity from power plants is curtailed, lights dim, factories close and people hunker down. Safety rules restrict otherwise popular winter sports."

A touchy point in our marriage: Anita ice skated. I didn't. She surprised me with a pair of skates to my pretended pleasure. Fearfully accompanying her to Central Park that winter, I

211

wobbled about slowly, full of dread. She did fine. I fell regularly. She mentioned it innocently only when I championed male superiority over the weaker sex.

"Morcot's food isn't grown outdoors. Summer heat destroys everything – people, too, explaining this planet's sluggish population growth. Nutrients are manufactured in blocks diluted in water into semi-liquid meals. The beverage of choice is water.

"Homespun clothing is made from a product like Thinsulate but thinner and warmer *or cooler.* All winter everyone wears a body-tight outfit made from it. When the government declares a water shortage, nobody bathes until it's over. Yech!

"There are no restaurants, no cows, steers or chickens. Meals are eaten at home; clothes are homemade. A big industry here is one-piece headgear with built-on goggles and earlaps that can't fall off. Before they were invented people went blind a few minutes after losing their goggles. If nobody was near enough to get them to shelter, they died.

"Family love is strong. Family size isn't governed; it's small because of tight quarters. Morcot is the first planet that *seems* to be an experiment. File notes complain that it must have been created to see if adversity built character.

"Morcots are Pragmatic Petes, (the name Anita used often to deride my atheism.)" "There's no formal religion but they have high ethical standards. Struggles that could make them enemies have made these people all for

212

one and one for all. Few survive burning summers and sub-zero winters longer than 65 years.

"Men process food or manufacture cloth, furniture and building materials from pulverized pulp. Forests also provide employment in felling, hauling, designing, finishing and selling wood products. Strict reforestation keeps their woodlands from giving out.

"Trade schools are for men only. Young girls stay with their mothers until thirteen whatevers. Boys start school at five and girls share housekeeping chores until they marry. Before their weddings, girls go out only to shop with mother." It struck me that Morcot offered an awful life for both sexes. I asked how boys and girls meet and fall in love. Anita said only, "They're lucky if they live long enough to marry."

Her channeling continued, "No poetry describes the stark beauty of Morcot's plateaus, mountains, enormous waterfalls, snow, ice formations and imposing forests. People are too busy surviving. No vacations or visits to relatives - just shuttling between home and work or imprisonment until work or marriage."

My impression was, Morcots should petition God for a better deal. Its people were hanging by their thumbs. Anita doubted my suggestion that they might be atoning for something awful their ancestors did. Nothing like that shows up in her notes."

She went on, "Morcot's much smaller than Earth, a big part of it under desert sun. No animals are mentioned, wild or domestic, which means no faithful pets *or* meat on the table to break the monotony of their diet."

Anita continued, "In the beginning, conditions were ideal. Seasons were mild. Supporting suns reflected temperate heat from a larger sun. But supporting suns blew up and away, weather deteriorated and Morcots were left to bear the insults of mortality.

> *"How I hope a loving throng was there to greet you*
> *And heal the insults of mortality.*
> *Life's balance seems an endless day without you,*
> *My faith threadbare confronting this necessity.*
>
> *"And yet you were so lovely in your passage -*
> *From autumn straight, your winter forfeited.*
> *That some imagined spring, some kind belief*
> *Could heal this loss, could mitigate this grief."*

By Amy Ober Flanders at her mother's memorial service

Morcot again: "Try to picture massive apartment houses centrally air conditioned and heated, with no windows to leak in extreme cold. Every apartment has its own atomic box to bridge server breakdowns. Boxes last generations before losing power.

"Central generators feed communities from isolated quarries where atomic cores are buried. Growing children learn never to handle the family's individual atomic box, used during outages or brownouts.

I doubt if that would have stopped Dody. Anita reported with mixed irritation and admiration that, from the time she became mobile, Dody dug up everything in the house,

214

examining, scattering, appraising and appropriating whatever appealed to her. If something was missing, the place to look for it was Dody's room.

Anita marveled at the tenacity of Morcot's citizens but didn't see why survival had to be so hard. "Maybe the Creator keeps them going because they're loving people. Maybe they're being studied for what the rest of us can learn from them."

I asked how they get to and from work. "Through heated tunnels. Bicycle paths run to the left of car lanes, sidewalks are to the right. Outdoor roads are safe for parts of summers and in milder winter periods. But forecasting's iffy. The cautious use tunnels."

I asked who's in charge. "A conservative government with no dictator or party labels. The leadership standard on Morcot is conservation."

What do they look like? Anita could say only that they have high color in their cheeks from the summer sun and outdoor winter exposure. I said toasting and freezing didn't sound like much of a life.

She pointed out, "Morcot must be a showcase for Spartan survival" and agreed that other planets have easier ways for people to be productive more comfortably. "But," she said, "Morcots are too busy to be unhappy, like the old Charlie Chaplin film about a speed-up society with no time out for joy or misery."

Morcot family life: "Government allows up to two children a family. Inbreeding is illegal. When parents can't agree on their children's mates, government chooses. In fact, for *every vital problem* there's a regulated solution."

I asked if Morcot had space travel. She said, "Nothing here flies but hardy birds."

My next question: "Do prospective mates date, nightclub, live together? Is there a marriage ceremony, a honeymoon?" Anita mentioned signed authorizations to mate and that couples live with her parents until the male works, when they get their own homes.

"There's nothing written about heartthrobs. Romance isn't mentioned in the files, or, for that matter, is there anything about women's rights. Women seem to consider themselves better off at home permanently."

I chewed on that overnight. Anita knew what was in my mind. "If I 'read' you, the planets are varied enough for you but the people seem too much alike for your taste. I believe God has one basic human blueprint that environments change some or a lot.

"Don't ask me why other peoples aren't dramatically different from Earth types. Different Earth environments develop different colors and characteristics. It's the same on all the planets." We moved on to the planet Nolar the next night.

"Experiment #5 was thrust (explained later) in 6,775. Who knows if it marks when Nolar was created or means something else? Nolar is another forbidding place, five major continents riddled by live volcanoes, steaming fogs and frequent eruptions.

"Seas and rivers, warm to boiling, are fed by hot springs bubbling up from the planet's superheated core. Hot water and gas from the same inner depths escape through river beds and volcanic cones. Volcanoes are harnessed to produce hot water and power.

"Nolar's five continents have broad hot channels between them – five parallel hot dogs in seas where hot water, gas and lava spew up regularly. People live in air-conditioned gas-tight glass brick apartment homes, entering and exiting through tightly insulated storm doors. The sun is seldom seen - hot mist, showers, dim days and dark nights prevail on all five continents.

"Nolar people live their lives close to where they're born. In-home hydroponic garden rooms grow their fruits and vegetables. There are no limits on killing free roving game, roasted in central grills over volcanic gas outlets. Gas also serves each family indoors, plus hot water for bathing, warm water for cleaning and tepid water for drinking. Ice refrigerators being primitive, neighbors divide and consume game meat before it spoils. Four is all one hydroponic garden can feed. No family is larger.

217

"A husband and wife produce two children *born with sexes undetermined.* At puberty, parents decide which will be male and which female. One duct is surgically opened and another closed, deciding masculinity or femininity. After that, girls wear long hair, boys crop theirs and selected couples are encouraged to 'fall in love.'

"Young marrieds are obligated to both sets of parents - to grow their food, cook for and clean both homes. At 'twenty-five,' couples are the heads of the households and roles reverse. Parents live with them, helping out until death at somewhere around forty. Life is short, and could be sweeter."

More about Nolar: "Thick forests and quarries feed vital lumbering and building operations. A family member works a day a week in the local mill or refinery, earning an equal share of lumber, glass bricks and construction materials – labor for products.

"Mating your own children is taboo. The boy next door marries the girl next door. They're educated at home. Parents tell their children what they know. That's it."

Nolar didn't strike me as an improvement on the earlier planets, the first one wrecked, one too cold, some with big uninhabitable areas, this one a leaky hot gas bag. My impression is that planet peopling needs help and I asked Anita, "How do Nolars get by with bad refrigeration?"

"Badly. They live off each day's yield. Leftovers aren't long spoiling."

I said, "It sounds monotonous and dangerous. Any desserts?"

She replied, "Not that I know of. There's no ice cream truck.

Anita used to marvel that Dody, an early expert in such matters, was waiting for the ice cream truck at the bottom of our hill in White Meadow Lake before anyone heard its clanging peal to the small fry to come and get it. Dody was also an expert in the brand names of automobiles before she could read. We never knew how.

Menus are no adventure in Nolar. Furniture, glass and materials for construction and repairs are cooperative efforts. There's no expansion plan, no coveting thy neighbor's wife or garden, not a mention of sweets – nothing you'd swap life on Earth for."

I mentioned that peaceful societies she described are too busy surviving to make war and indulge in popular evils. "Maybe God improves us best with hardships."

Anita said, "Something must explain His thinking with each experiment, but these files state facts without philosophy and I can't tell you anything that isn't here."

I asked, "What if two kids fall in love but both choose the same sex?"

"They can't make that choice. The law says, one male and one female, even balance, zero population growth. Boys don't bunk together, or girls. It would upset the need to keep the population from growing or shrinking."

She added, "Glass homes aren't built for remodeling. When one is damaged by a meteor or volcanic eruption its encasement is replaced exactly."

I asked if Nolar's five continents had the same glass houses, trees or whatever. "They're all alike. And there's nothing about town protest meetings or elections, radical movements, youthful rebellions. Life is family. There's no dissent. I miss suspense, pursuit, men sweeping women off their feet." Nolar, too, seems to be stuck in low gear. They miss everything in life that builds beautiful memories.

I had a life before Anita but began loving it when I fell in love with her. In summer 1942 when we met I had no car. We took the IRT train to Rockaway Park and changed into bathing suits in a mildewed boardwalk bathhouse. She later accused me of taking her there to get a good look at her body, which I neither affirmed nor denied. We swam, had lunch on the beach and stretched out on a blanket. I read to her from a book of poems, "Elephant Up a Tree," by Hendrick Willem Van Loon. Anita loved it and I adored that sunny, brown-eyed beauty whose eyes sparkled and whose soul melded with mine on the beach in Rockaway Park. It was the first of many trips to the ocean throughout our marriage. Our children and Dody's learned to love the beach as much as we did. Thank you, God.

Next let's get down to Earth.

Experiment #6 turned out to be our world, Planet Earth. "Its code number is 6443. "Earth was born in a big bang with a big ricochet. It hurled away from an exploding sun, took shape as it spun and found a new home in its present sun's orbit.

"I'm not going to give you a big picture of our planet, but nobody named Adam or Eve begot its people. God put Earth humans down in a way different from the earlier planets. Life forms on Experiments #1 through #5 began with attracting amoebas that merged. On Earth streams were stocked with fish. Some eventually adapted to dry land. From them, shrewd, unintelligent humans and animals evolved as God planned.

"There was debate in heaven over how much intelligence potential to give Earth's humans. The heart of the Earth experiment was that, if man evolved from lower forms, he would empathize with his lesser ancestors and all would live in peace. When it didn't turn out that way, God decided the imperfections were creative failures and that *He* needed to adjust living beings until they truly loved each other. He works on that here to this day.

"Enough about what you more or less know. Whoever calls our ancestors savages is a pot calling a kettle black. The ferocity of today's mass murder and destruction was unimagined on Earth by its early savages.

"Maybe I haven't made a big enough point of this - that while His peopling experiments have all disappointed God, some are more peaceful than others. Earth isn't one of the peaceful ones. But the Creator hasn't given up on any planet's population yet."

Anita finally caught up with the man Mr. Kincaide said could help us understand the number code of the peopled planets. She wrote, "His name is Marc with a "c". He's an aboriginal, one of the people *created here* to assist in God's work. There are thousands like him. Without ever being on a peopled world, Marc helped plan them all.

"A senior advisor now, he studied sciences, geography and nature and worked on techniques for developing humans from lesser forms. Marc will drop in to talk to you."

Later: "Marc says the universes *were* deliberately set up to isolate peopled planets and when humans can teach and learn without being stoned or worse, communication among the planets will begin. A blueprint for removing the barriers exists.

"I asked him if a planet might discover extra-universal travel on its own. He said it wouldn't happen until the restraints are removed."

Next letter: my time was 11:28 p.m. when I met Marc. She began, "Marc has been here forever or so, counseling with God and other creationists. The plan all along was to people ten planets. After each was populated they designed changes for the next."

Anita introduced Marc who began, "Norman, our experiments *haven't* matured as foreseen. God no longer forces change. Humans make their destinies, select leaders, often foolishly - or leaders impose themselves. But humans weren't created to be unequal.

"Too often His love is unfelt or poorly defined on the planets. Earth is one on which love is verbalized, as hate is; but your most eloquent couples can fall out of love. If it isn't for life, can it be love? God is masculine, though I feel your Joan of Arc would have made a marvelous God. Women on the average are godlier than men."

Anita's my candidate for the job. I'm filled with remorse that what she tried to teach her macho husband about God didn't sink in until after she died. When we drove down from Oregon to California, our ancient Hudson needed new pistons (again) in Red Bluff. The delay made me AOL (absent over leave). That night I fell apart. The Navy, we'd been drilled to understand, would accept any good excuse for lateness unless you missed your ship. I didn't know yet that my home at sea was still in a shipyard. I did know we wouldn't get out of Red Bluff for two days. Anita sat up with me all the first night and soothed courage back into me to face my fate. When we reached Terminal Island two days AOL, the duty officer ended my dread by changing my arrival date.

Marc continued, "I had early interest in governance and universal astronomy. I study the sciences of the planets. Earth is more advanced than all but two.

"We define true religion as belief in one God, demonstrated by behavior in His image. He doesn't punish non-believers or see profit as an excuse for

223

cruelty and killing. We try to promote fair play for and by every human species. We see the city as natural order on par with rural areas, small communities and open spaces where few live. We seek to perfect equality, respect and equal benefits for all people.

"But cupidity overpowers honor. Regime after regime still wastes humans of potential in wars that squander many to benefit few. The meek do not inherit the earth. They bear the brunt of its pain and death by exploitation.

"Weaponry was not created here. God does not favor victor or loser, though both claim His support. God envisions inhabited worlds in which all live in harmony.

"Experiment #1, Enistor, received intense study to satisfy us that colonies could succeed outside of heaven. Then that planet suffered a deadly natural disaster not fully understood. The rest require improvement. With eternity to work, we go forward.

"That said, Norman, I will address the planetary numbers. I know you haven't memorized them, so I will give you their common basis. The numbers mark not when peopling began but when thrust operations, which preceded habitation, ended.

"Thrust is the best English word I know to describe how we provide universes with solar systems, microorganisms, minerals, water, gases and the other resources impacting each other to foster and sustain life once a planet is habitation-ready. I urge patience until you understand this."

With that Marc turned me back to Anita.

The next night Anita asked what I made of Marc. I said he wasn't so hard to follow but thrust didn't mean much more than chucking it all out there. Anita promised a better definition if she could get one. I asked what Marc looked like.

She replied, "Hollywood would cast him as a Roman senator too benign to kill Caesar. He's clean shaven, *looks* smart, handsome and dignified." I didn't know then that I would hear from Marc again (See 'Afterword') and that he'd jolt me into amending my lifelong antagonism against Irish Catholics.

Next night, Anita said she queried Marc again. "You have thrust right. The numbers we're struggling with mark off the intervals between thrust dates." I see no point in dating thrusts when nothing in heaven seems to have a date, but who asked me?"

Anita continued, "Planets selected for peopling already had habitats most favorable to living. To be sure of it, God and His advisors delivered − by thrusting − vast quantities of pure oxygen and nitrogen in solid and fluid form, of life-supporting minerals, fortified loam and plant life insuring human genesis and survival.

"Marc says males, conceived of first, were alone in the plan until the problem of propagation arose. Woman came not from Adam's rib but from the decision that men should not propagate themselves and raise children alone.

"Conferences and papers outlined what should or could happen once life began. Man and woman were intended to love each other, to make survival worth the struggle. Pleasure was added to sexual intercourse, insuring future generations. Population building aside, sexual appetites created considerable unintended mischief."

Then Anita came back to thrust: "With every foreseeable need and problem addressed, a massive movement of materiel soaked each selected planet with sustained heavy rains of nutrients, seeds, chemicals and minerals, flooding them with life-enabling and supporting raw materials. To an extent it was hit or miss. This was compensated for by thrusting an overabundance of everything needed to establish life.

"The technique improved as they went along. Mistakes were corrected. Marc recalled that nutrients tended to run off in #1, creating water and food supply problems that had to be fixed. Energy from Nolar's hot core was tapped after killing frosts on Morcot nearly depopulated it. They went overboard with the hot water, but did better on Earth, with subterranean supplies, hot *and* cold, to stock its aquifers and reservoirs.

"Marc said that if the word thrust troubles you, use your own. He prefers thrust because massive delivery through the vastness of space isn't as simple as dropping supplies from airplanes. Topographical, temperature and wind current variations cause distribution irregularities. Sandy soil retains little nourishing to people. Useful nutrients leach away in rocky areas, too, over-enriching rivers and oceans and spawning deserts."

Before Marc got our attention, we were discussing Earth, the first planet on which human life evolved from simpler life forms. First primates and humans grunted and snarled at each other. Their brains improving, descendants evolved into unique races.

Nobody we knew was as unique as our Belgian friend Jean Demain. A former spy in the Belgian underground, she was the fascinating main speaker at a United Jewish Appeal function Anita attended at the Waldorf-Astoria. I met Jean that evening when I came home from work. Anita had approached the tall, imposing bombshell after her electrifying speech, embraced her and said, "I have to know you." And there she was in our living room in Stuyvesant Town having a cocktail with my good wife.

Jean graduated from exotic foreigner to lifelong friend in a few hours as we learned about her life as a spy. A blonde blue-eyed Catholic darling of occupying Nazi officers, she aided the underground resistance to Belgium's captors until the Nazis grew suspicious and her compatriots spirited her out of Belgium. UJA welcomed her powerful personality and fascinating war stories to fire up financial support for Israel.

Jean mesmerized Dody, operating her dimpled baby arms as she sang the words to "La Petite Marionette" on nights that she stayed with us between out of town speaking tours and Jean and Anita talked all hours like teenagers at a slumber party. We still loved Anita's "find," long after Jean died of an intractable neuromuscular disease.

The last time we visited her, Anita sat alongside her floor mat in the home high on a hill overlooking San Francisco. Jean shared it with her husband Aldo Scaglioni, former WWII partisan and professor of Italian at a number of American Universities. We knew that day we'd never see her again and it broke Anita's heart.

I later worked on a book of biographies, one of them Jean Demain's. It was a labor of love. I knew all the subjects personally, loved most of them. Only Norman Corwin among them became truly famous in his time. (He was lauded in 2006 when a short subject about him titled, "A Note of Triumph," won an Oscar.)

Anita had nothing to add about Planet Earth so we turned to Storic.

The description began, "Experiment #7, Storic, is coded 5221. It's more advanced than Earth in some ways, behind us in others. The formula for creating life there was the same as on Earth – simpler life forms evolving into creatures and humans.

"Storic's settled areas are divided into neat planned population cores surrounded by industrial rings, in turn girt by extensive farmlands. Government observation towers at high points keep track of their skies and lowlands. Industry is isolated to retard pollution affecting residences and farms.

"High-speed railroads connect factory, farm and bedroom communities. Centralized power distribution systems operate, as people say these days, twenty-four seven. Unlike the USA where farms get larger and fewer, great numbers of small Storic farms produce all year round. Agricultural sciences continually improve the taste, quality and variety of fresh and preserved foods. In that they're ahead of any other planet.

"Fresh game from hunting preserves is available under strict sports rules. Only crossbows, bows and arrows and hand-held projectiles called ferrocks are allowed for hunting. A ferrock is a spear or lance with a spring blade release.

"Storic has five independent continents that warred until their women revolted, like in Greek drama. Women were imprisoned and forced into slavery.

But nothing daunted them. Men couldn't imprison or kill them all and survive. The wars stopped.

"Once the stalemate ended, women pressed for and won treaties outlawing future warfare and tyranny. Planet-wide pacts commit the full resources of Storic governments to crush individuals or groups circumventing the treaties.

"A thriving air industry provides high-speed travel. People retire on pensions at fifty-five. Jobs generally last until retirement. Competition for work went out with war. This isn't a matriarchal society. Men and women divide responsibilities equally. By law, family heads own their assets and properties jointly.

"Men and women choose careers and stick with them. There's been no killing since society came down hard on murder or attempted murder with the death penalty. Lesser criminals are banished for life to prison colonies.

"Criminals manufacture products accepted and paid for on all continents, enabling them to import products they can't make or raise themselves. There's no second chance for convicted criminals. One strike and they're out of mainstream society for life."

Anita wrote that Storic has nuclear energy know-how, but it's not in use yet. Scientists are trying to find safe ways to develop and use it.

"The sun, higher than Earth's, gives off gentler heat and light. Winter is mild. There's no torrid zone. The combination of the sun's rapid course and Storic's orbit provides an equal number of days and nights.

"Parents vote on classroom curricula. Schools provide normal and specialized education, to bring appropriate learning to the bright, normal and retarded."

Abe and Lily Rosenblum had one bright child (Anita) and one exceptionally bright child (Robbie). Abe's early policy about household expenses was, "If I have it in my pocket, we can spend it. If not, no" Robbie, at about six, developed the skill of rifling his father's pockets and wallet, squirreling away what he found. Anita loved telling about the day Abe said they couldn't afford something and Robbie produced the money to buy it.

"Families are rewarded for saving. The highest savers earn the highest pensions. Storic grasshoppers," Anita wrote, "don't fiddle, summer or winter. They get into solid businesses for better pensions and probably take violin lessons when they retire.

"The five independent continents have identical governance codes. Officials serve two-year terms. Few office holders run again. Mandatory but poorly paid public service is a drag on pension earnings, depressing retirement allotments.

"On Storic, it seems, there's someone for everyone. Newlyweds live with the girl's parents, who get tax abatements for their expenses for a set period, after which a couple is expected to be self-sufficient. Parents may still help, but tax support ends.

"Young workers begin as apprentices. The government pays them for a set period. From then on, employers pay their wages. Workers that employers don't keep are apprenticed again. Low beginner pay inclines apprentices to succeed and be kept on.

"Industrial and commercial firms have company paid employee training courses. Students applying for advanced studies pass stringent tests to qualify for scholarships.

"Healthy habits have people averaging over a hundred years. There are few 'bad' births. By law, damaged babies are disposed of after birth. Only perfect babies are acceptable, but mildly retarded children are allowed to work up to their capabilities."

Anita reported that Storics aren't highly emotional people and don't use drugs, tobacco or alcohol. They enjoy work. With parental help for perhaps two years and job subsidies for half of that, careers are chosen with care. So are mates. A couple that can't get along can separate but if they marry again, they're on their own financially."

"They believe in a Creator and life after death. But there's no church. Like early Gnostics, Quakers and Deists, Storics look for God within. Storic religions once menaced people with damnation if they withheld extortionate tithes. You picked a church to get the others to stop hounding you. When clergies instituted punishment by death for non-payment of tithes, after a bloody time, church militias were defeated and proselytizing became illegal."

I asked, "What about art?"

"Continents have their own painting tastes, styles and art schools. Still life and portraits dominate, reminiscent of 19th Century English portraits, landscapes and seascapes. Each generation has its own culture. Pop music to symphonies to no music at all seems to keep their adherents happy.

That reminded me of young Turks Anita and I saw in action at the Concertgebouw in Amsterdam in the Seventies. Protesters stopped the concert with noisemakers to express frustration over entrenched composers' domination of the program selection process. Nearby Dutch seat holders interpreted the goings-on for us bewildered tourists.

"Storics have little creative ferment. They accept art forms as they do everything else in their lives. It takes huge outrages to rouse them. They fought for peace and freedom, but instead of using their victory to create alternative lifestyles, the governors and governed are contented with status quo gently warmed over.

"Storic scientists have theorized TV but are in no hurry to develop it. They feel radio gives them what they need and heavily censored movies offer uncomplicated diversion. Enough money's around, but nobody dreams big enough to push for growth projects. Politicians don't promise big. People don't have big expectations.

"Sports emphasize healthy bodies, not competition. There are no opposing teams. Nobody wins. In jogging, running, bicycling, walking or swimming, the goal is *finishing*. There's no baseball, football or tennis but there's something like golf with no scoring.

"Marginal notes declare that life is great on this planet. A dissenting comment complained that nobody on Storic has ambition."

Chapter 48: Virch

Anita began, "Experiment #8 was thrust at 5014. Its people call it Ordus, but I'll use its name in heaven. Virch outstripped all other planets in technology, invention and creativity before being reduced to scattered clusters of mutants. Its people fell from a remarkably advanced state of civilization to primitive conditions in one day.

"To begin with, they're all islanders. No one land area is as big as Australia; they're a nation of small countries like lily pods on White Meadow Lake. Life is rudimentary now. People use clubs for defense. They no longer have the formidable weaponry they did. They *were* highly developed and boasted superior minds and achievements. A small number of fortified islands were their power and policing bases. Industries flourished but most people didn't. Industrial conglomerates ruled Virch.

"In thickly settled cities on the larger islands, trade was lively, markets abundant. Everywhere high skills produced sophisticated products as states federated to control industry, wages, inventions, import, export and living conditions.

"Federation leadership kept everyone in line under the threat of death. Revolt against the power centers seemed impossible, but a time came when key workers and professionals began disappearing with their families from homes and workplaces.

"More and more top-performing technocrats, scientists and physicians vanished. Equipment, weapons and a large amount of a yellow substance called fornate (uranium?) disappeared with them.

"With that, Federation leaders dispatched fleets and armies to find and destroy them, but search parties failed to track them down. When the search was abandoned, small hit and run raids on the establishment began. More people, arms and equipment disappeared. Federation power bases armed themselves to the teeth. Bombers patrolled the skies day and night. Dissidents remained invisible. Stealthy raids accelerated.

"The rebels," Anita wrote, "finally went public. In Axtil, the primary power capital, demands appeared on the desks of high-level administrators. Relatives of missing people were rounded up and killed in a ruthless show of force.

"But nothing stopped the shadow war or its growing damage to Federation assets. Dissidents issued a deadline for Federation to dissolve or see the Axtil business district vaporized. That was greeted by derision until a note warned that the district would be destroyed and its people killed if not evacuated overnight.

"The threat was ignored. The district was vaporized. Over two hundred thousand died instantly and survivors soon after. Destruction was total.

"Then the unseen attackers advised that, in two shantils (whatever they measure), all Federation state buildings in Axtil would be vaporized. Federation answered with fleets of aircraft equipped with, I suppose, nuclear warheads.

Thousands executed saturation bombing on random locations, aimed to bring dissidents to their knees.

"But Federation miscalculated. The bombs set off a firestorm that engulfed virtually all of Virch. Only shreds of life survived in isolated areas sideswiped by raging wind driven fire. Deformed survivors barely cling to their language and culture on a planet that turned against and destroyed itself.

Now, in ragged communes, its people range for food and water safe to eat and drink. They occupy caves and mud shelters where cruel leaders controlled a technologically exceptional world that was toppled in a day."

"Experiment #9 is called Orinth. Its thrust code is 4892. This planet, too, has developed beyond Earth in many ways. Orinth, larger than Earth, has a solar system with no moon. Magnetic fields coming from its core regulate tidal flow. There used to be one large landmass as Earth was when it began. Orinthians believe that pre-historic catastrophes caused tidal waves and explosions that split the mass in two.

"The continents warred constantly until agreements were negotiated to cooperate in managing their peoples and economies. During the peace that followed, technology created robotic machinery that eliminated thousands of jobs once assigned to humans. Civil war broke out against seldom-seen overseers, rich from labor squeezed too hard.

"The leadership had been so confident in its local guard systems that there were no armies to put down the rebellion. Leaders were ousted. Their preserves and properties confiscated, they were put to work with little bloodshed.

"Committees were created to oversee manufacturing, commerce and monetary matters. Trade strengthened. A uniform scale of values was introduced. Pacts were signed equalizing prosperity on both continents. Inflation was overcome by printing new money honored on both continents and by instituting uniform controlled pricing.

"Democratic governments and voting systems emerged. Moderately paid elected officials truly represent the people. Robots were scrapped. Unemployment was eliminated. Early retirement keeps the work force young. Everybody participates in profits. There are no second-class citizens, no wealthy, no poor.

"Science and medicine have made enormous advances. Government is supported by taxes scaled to ability to pay. There's no bankruptcy. Successful balancing of living and working conditions has socialized the planet.

"New discoveries are universal property. Diseases that used to plague Orinth have disappeared. Legal abortions are as common as marriage. The mean life span for women is 102 common years, whatever they are, and for men 98.

Anita described Orinth's homes as futuristic by our standards. "Built-in storage facilities and automated full-time silent central air suction systems keep them clean.

"An invention called worsal, developed here, disposes of leftovers. Everything from stale food to broken cooling units and overage vehicles is compressed, solidified and cut into bricks used for building roads and other public works. Smaller worsal home and business units reduce everything fed into them, divert used water for purification and make paper, plastic and metal blocks for municipal pickup and conversion.

"There are no volcanic eruptions or earthquakes, though the core of the planet is extremely hot. Weather-wise, storms are *reliably diverted* to where rainwater is needed by manipulating gradient winds and redistributing precipitation.

239

"Liquid worsal runoff is piped to purification tanks, made potable and cycled back into the water system. Impurities are drawn off for chemical analysis and reuse or disposal. Great public works projects, always in progress, eliminate underemployment.

"Big government-run entertainment campuses, like heaven's, offer live sports, films, video, live stage performances, circuses, concerts, ballet and opera. Eight events take place, day and evening at each campus. Every art form is government supported.

"Typical homes are apartment buildings. Private estates were razed after the uprising and replaced by treed avenues of four-story one, two and three bedroom apartments. No elevators. Walkup is popular health exercise.

"If people become disabled, they're moved to ground level apartments. When parents and grandparents are too old to work, they move in with children, getting the family preference for low floors. Orinth pay scales include living allowances for the disabled. When the young leave home, a share of family savings goes with them. Government stipends are added as their new families grow.

"Medical centers, too, resemble apartment houses. Larger business areas maintain satellite hospital staffs and facilities to accommodate minor medical needs.

"There's one religion, the worship of God, I'm sure ours. He is sensed as a good spirit and is loved as the head of all families. He's believed to have a goddess wife. There are no churches, but lay sermons, broadcast by radio, are very popular.

"The able-bodied go to amusement complexes. Transmission facilities send live shows and movies from amusement centers to shut-ins.

"Orinth holds elections every four years. A leader, council of eleven and a unicameral parliament are voted in. Workers and executives draw the same pay. When society has higher expectations, wages and productivity go up."

Anita reported that finances are in the hands of a board, appointed for life, which oversees non-profit banks that guard savings for fees and pay no interest. There's no stock market. The major purpose of government is to promote production, oversee growth and distribution of food products and raising domestic animals for food.

Land is tax-free to contributors of food and livestock above their needs. Trees and flowers are abundant in city parks. Flowers can be taken home when they bloom.

Anita's favorite flowers were lilacs. Her big brown eyes lit up and there were extra kisses for me every April when florists had them. Our second White Meadow home had two lilac bushes. The house was filled with their fragrance and her pleasure in them.

Finally on Orinth, Anita reflected, "It's no utopia, but there are no neuroses – people are contented. Every home has an electric car, which it's forbidden to drive alone. In rush hours five people occupy one vehicle, at off times at least two. Familiar?

241

"They have separate airplane and rocket ports whose carriers fly great distances safely. Aircraft routinely travel faster than the speed of sound. Conventional and rocket planes drop smoothly into mobile wrapping beds that slide them to soft safe landings.

"Women are plain, men handsome. Women pursue, men accept. Both sexes work to fifty and retire. Day care centers supervise the young if no grandparents are available. Work is nine 'hours' a day with lunch pills for bridge nourishment and no interruption in work until the evening meal.

"Factories and commercial establishments provide special workplaces for the unmarried, exactly as many men as women to a section. You meet the girl or boy of your dreams there. Larger firms have chapels where couples marry on the spot, then go back to work. There's no word for honeymoon. On Orinth productivity rules supreme! "

That left us only one more peopled planet to plumb.

Anita's notes on the last peopled planet: "Experiment #10's thrust code is 4874. Take it or leave it."

"Ornus is another large land mass surrounded by oceans whose currents travel counter-clockwise in seas with no ice at either pole. A temperate sun moves north and south, distributing rain without flooding or dry spells. Speedy ocean-going ferries, tankers, freighters and pleasure craft follow the current, circum-navigating the continent.

"Ornus is shaped like a watermelon standing on one end. All of it is habitable. Wheat crops grow nearly to the poles north and south, two crops a year, broken by a mild winter solstice. Ornus's wheat fields are the planet's breadbasket.

"Agricultural sciences developed disease-free wheat, corn, rye and other grains. Flours are apparently never bleached. A low calorie product called ficca, a nutritious natural sweetener, is grown, powdered unprocessed and used widely.

"People average 150 years with few debilitating diseases. Hospitals treat mostly accidents. Human immune systems are exceptional. Fleets of flying ambulances ferry patients from rural areas. At speeds faster than light, nobody's far from a hospital.

"Cauterizing and immediately replanting human flesh is a technique for repairing open wounds. Fast calcifying agents repair broken or damaged bones.

Damaged muscles and blood vessels are replaced by implanting quick-fix vein and artery substitutes.

"Nearly everyone lives reasonably well. However, livestock prices are high. Most people are vegetarians. Meatless dieters popularly supplement with murniss, a protein grain that makes patties good for any meal (veggie burgers?).

"Compulsory dietary laws keep the planet's people healthy. Inspectors pour in when diseases break out, to identify and eliminate them. Effective cures benefit the whole planet, because there's one federal government seeing to the needs of the people.

"Parliament consists of 400 city delegates. By a fuzzy formula, rural areas pay city officials to represent them. Elected officials serve five years. Government service is mandatory. Office holders greet the end of their single terms with celebrations.

"Parliament appoints its leaders and committees. Plenary sessions vote every five working days. Ornus has the only 100% honest government in the peopled planets.

"Science and engineering have developed high-speed overland trucks, trains and rocket craft that run on solid fuel. Spacecraft continually probe their universe.

"They believe they're the only inhabited planet, but a theory increasingly popular is that their universe has boundaries decreed by God. They speculate widely on why that's so. They theorize other universes, but doubt any are peopled.

"Having come that far, the government discourages religious differences and provides public pulpits for theologians who see God's hand in their creation and warn against lack of gratitude for the good life they have.

"Heavy industries attract workers with their own training schools. Retirement is mandatory at eighty of their years. Culturally, this is an advantaged planet, with fine arts, libraries, cinema, radio and television, live drama, musicals, opera and dance. They also have Directed Fancy, a popular way to review and interpret dreams and daydreams.

"Libraries have no controversial books. There are no notes on how any civilizations developed. They believe they sprang, full-grown, from the head of a journeyman Zeus who moved on after finishing the job.

"Boy- girl romances are tightly controlled. Parents and government must approve marital decisions. Young people don't seem unhappy with it. For making babies, men and women test for genetic compatibility, marriage and birth prospects. Artificial sperm is inseminated to create 'ideal' children – there are no offspring from do-it-yourself pregnancies. The process succeeds physically but family relationships are shaky.

"Younger generations resign from families, maybe because families are run like businesses. There are no costs above taxes. Family income is paid by the community and taxed right back. There's neither opportunity nor incentive to get rich. Because surpluses go to the government, in bad times government underwrites family needs. It balances out.

I asked, "Do Ornus types look like us?"

Anita said, "Ornus types compare reasonably with the rest of us. Only Virch, the planet of the severe atomic wipeout, has radically mutilated mutants."

I asked, "How do people dress on Ornus? "

Anita answered, "They manufacture material foreign to Earth, lightweight and flexible, blended wood fiber fabrics in varying weight and thickness. Polar winters call for heavier dress. Northern and southern farms subject to strong winds and lower temperatures use the heavy fabrics, too. These materials suit all dress codes, formal or informal. Open neck shirt collars sound like open collar garments worn in India."

Anita dressed me. I'd have worn the same outfit every day of the year if she didn't know my sizes better than I did, bring home clothes from Alexander's, Klein's, Orbach's and the May Company for me to try on and patiently exchange them when they didn't fit. She laid out my wardrobe for office, travel or pleasure every day. When my income climbed, Anita found a man named Mr. Silver who came to the house, measured me for suits, jackets and slacks and looked at Anita when he talked to me about selecting cloths for suiting. God bless my love for all reasons, seasons and Mr. Silver.

Finally on Ornus: "Both sexes are six feet or taller. Shorter strains were eliminated, as was obesity when they realized it shortened life. Health regimens are popular. Animals are taboo for human consumption, but useful as pets, for hides, bone materials and medical experiments. Laboratories raise test animals humanely and grow the feeds they consume. "Nobody resents vivisection, but nobody wears animal furs."

I asked, "How would you describe their speech?"

"I can't. Accents of other planets are sometimes described but not recorded. My educated reading box translates languages but doesn't answer questions. Unlike other planets, Ornus has only one language. They call it ornus (no initial capital) and also call their planet and universe Ornus with a capital O.

"They have dialects. References to the unschooled speech of politicians from rural locales mimic urban derision of Earth's frontiersmen. I didn't mention it before, but women govern on equal footing with men here. That's nice." That completes the abridged versions of Anita's reports on the peopled planets.

PART SEVEN

Anita took on a new job, leaving Receiving for Human Betterment. What she found there helped us decide how we will spend our afterlife together. The idea took root as Anita channeled about groups seeking ways to stop and reverse environmental influences that degrade human character and life. What she taught me made me impatient to work in a place I used to think didn't exist.

Taking on new jobs was no problem for Anita — dental assistant, preschool teacher and starry-eyed housewife, face flushed with pleasure when I raved over her Sampson Navy dinners and delicious home made pies from fruit we picked in nearby orchards. When she taught kindergarten and ran a pre-school at Tongue Point, Oregon, she baked more pies — of huge blackberries and salmonberries we picked next to Highway 30, the main road splitting Tongue Point from its housing area.

Later in San Pedro and Hollywood she was a part-time waitress, then worked in a haberdashery and was a seamstress, then a saleswoman at the May Company. When our daughters were old enough, she returned to sales at Arnold Constable and later worked as a librarian, researcher, part time meeting planner, puzzle editor and full time critic of my character, deportment and writing.

The destructive impact of environment and evolution on the human condition led her to report that debating creation versus evolution is silly. From heaven's perspective, three forces in perpetual conflict are God, evolution and environment.

"Living loses ground to evolutionary and environmental erosion. God wants every person to live, love and be happy. As evolution and environment challenge the peopled planets, He works to repair cyclical erosion with cyclical restoration, a job that's become harder on some planets because of uncontrolled pollution."

Change of subject: "We have total sexual equality in heaven. Single people here commit to each other out of respect, love or desire for companionship. Here there are no primal urges, no passionate impulses. Women in heaven curl a lip at planetary sex that yields mostly one-sided satisfaction.

"God doesn't condone abuse or abusive sex, *nor hold that sex is for reproduction only*. Do AIDS, syphilis and gonorrhea come from God's disapproval? Environment, evolution, ignorance and dangerous choices spread those infectious diseases, not God."

Then this: "Earliest planets originally had telepathic communication as we have it here. They forfeited it by misuse, as surely as evolution took the dinosaurs away."

And: "Our task, not just His, is to make heaven's human betterment programs environment-proof. A few generations of glued-on goodness would make improvement permanent. Teams of biochemists work for God, creating elixirs to thrust above the worlds, inhaled chemicals that will eventually make people honest, forthright and ready to love each other in spite of environment or evolution."

250

"Though people reincarnate prepared to live by His standards, battered by environment, many lose the way. When ideal human relations exist on the planets permanently, survival stresses won't reverse pre-reincarnation purification."

"We're born into each life without evil. We're decent humans when environment allows it. We stray when it doesn't. In the event of complete dissolution of civilization, God or people themselves will eradicate the unregenerate along with the innocent. If He has a neo-Passover plan to liquidate the bad and spare the good, it's not written down in our libraries. Meanwhile, it's a good thing God isn't short-tempered."

More: "Unchecked environmental change produces more bad than good. It's a sad paradox when former liberals in your world become nouveaucrats pandering to the rich. The godly exist on every planet, standing apart from the selfish who thrive off their societies any way they can. If cruelty and selfishness never change, I fear humanity *will* one day be destroyed or self-destruct."

Then this: "God doesn't see human labor as expendable, nor does He approve of slavery, racial strife, war or murder. Yet wealth and power shackle, exploit and subvert whole nations. God blesses nobody who abuses power. In paradise His truth flourishes without sectarian or political manipulation."

That led me to ask, "Does any religion speak for God?"

She replied, "Most speak for Him part-time. Quakers, Ethical Culturists, Deists and many Gnostics love and respect God without editing and inspire followers without contrived dogmas threatening hell for dissent. Comparative religion courses here indict every long-established denomination claiming to be the only voice of God when its clerics subvert Him with fearsome fiction presented as His word.

"They have been trained to believe their texts. Pious masqueraders skew God's will, attack contradictory voices and use their pulpits to enforce their wills."

I asked Anita again why people continue praying to God when so many have nothing to show for it. Anita answered obliquely. "Did you pray for me to get well?"

"I did even though I didn't believe in God."

Her rejoinder was, "Didn't you see the irony of it?"

"I do now. But prayer hasn't brought you back to me."

"Hasn't it?" She reminded me that our channel was doing fine by us and that people come back to life by prayer in fiction and movies, but seldom in real life. She cited near-death experiences when, at or beyond the brink, some return to life; but, she said, "I didn't have that option because you need a working liver to be eligible."

In early 1990 Bill Ober frowned at a CAT scan of her liver. Telltale spots were everywhere. He said to us, "Surgery is not an option." Until that moment, we had hope. As at

252

our wedding, Anita's hands were icy cold. But I insisted on a futile search for options. We exhausted them and Anita, too, in two weeks. Then we waited.

Continuing Anita's letters: "Humans should fear God deciding evolutionary and environmental corruption can't be repaired. One planet's permanently destroyed and another barely survives. Not God but humans may end the experiments called life.

"I'm not hopeful enough to say, 'don't worry.' If no divine or human force deliberately destroys a planet, accident, tidal floods - any environmental disaster could produce or magnify forces to shatter more worlds."

Anita continued, "Any time after conception, environment may counterattack. Non-human elements may wipe out a planet. Even so, I still believe we can unite to overcome destruction of our worlds."

To break into Anita's two-edged speculation, I have to point out how her dire prophecy was followed by words of hope. She truly had a unique talent for coupling negativism with enthusiasm and as she learned, to express herself better and better. Having stolen the spotlight, I want one more moment to tell you and Anita, for the record, that I have never stopped being grateful for what brought and kept us together, even after death wrenched her from me.

Anita continued to talk about human betterment group activity and I've gathered together here much of what she passed along in the last year or two:

"One team wants to modify weather patterns, harness tidal waves, hurricanes, typhoons, droughts, earthquakes, floods, blizzards, famines, epidemics and other vicious vagaries of nature. Reversing destructive phenomena is considered possible. We tinker on paper and in the laboratory until there's peer consensus to conduct trials that seldom succeed. Every accepted idea is written up in detail, every foreseeable implication of a new project is debated. Too much is at stake for frivolous experimentation.

"Significant improvements cooked up here have typically been long projects. Meanwhile, on planet after planet, *human invention sometimes takes the lead.* We see that often where there are breakthroughs in medicine and pharmacology research."

In one moment of weakness, I confessed having doubts about the eventual triumph of human betterment, which I first trumpeted as work for us to do. I wrote that thoughts rolling around in my head for encouraging ethics, equality and morality are the same ones that have been tossed around for millennia without results. "If the big religions can't get it done, if heaven can't do it, maybe we're blowing in the wind."

254

Her answer was, "There's no deadline here. We believe not whether but when."

My concerns about biting off more than we could chew didn't last, but even Anita once fretted, "Suddenly trusting societies *would* be meat for unrepentant opportunists. I'm tempted to believe humanity won't improve without direct divine intervention. But let's keep looking for ideas. Nay saying changes naught."

"A lot of Earth people who support human betterment don't mean equality for women, who, too, are Gentile, Jew, White, Black, Red and Yellow. When ethics, morals and intentions improve, women's rights must. When I asked, nobody seemed to know any committee doing *that* work."

Later she found a small group. "The leader is from Storic. After I explained our interest, the two women and three men invited me to stay. They want to recruit missionary legions to return to planets as true soldiers preaching equality of the sexes."

Anita wasn't confident that five people could muster armies to change the worlds. But, she said, dedicated idealists refining human betterment theories want millions to join their group and some to think up new steps to equalize the roles of the sexes.

We were never big joiners. The radio network writers' contract put me in The Radio Writers Guild and Author's League. I did become chairman of the Radio Division, Progressive Citizens of America, supporting Henry Wallace for President in 1948, but we never joined his

Progressive Party. Anita signed up for the Town & Village Chapter of Women's American

ORT but resigned when she was pressured to run for national office. It would have meant too

much time away from her family.

We later became Democrats. That was it, except for our White Meadow Lake car pool

and a toothless tontine Arnold Goren, Jack Soskin and I agreed to - to outlive each other. Arnold

and I are still here at this writing, with our friend Gil Tint as part of the overripe triumvirate,

fighting it out over breakfast with gusto when our dander's up.

Anita kept learning about new programs. "Groups occasionally have joint meetings to blend their ideas into one plan. I'll familiarize myself with as many as I can."

Later: "I met five scientists exploring ways to strengthen agricultural economies by improving soils, developing new foods and better storage facilities, restarting spent farmlands and containing attacks on farm acreage by commercial predators. Technology and starvation are in a race that starvation is winning in many countries."

More on reform: "A group exploring climate management to improve human behavior bore out that, outside of heaven, exposure to any prolonged weather pattern, good or bad, corrodes the spirit. Now they're working on a program to modify seasons with extra suns for better heat and rain distribution to make crops more cost-efficient."

My opinion was that programs like those aren't solutions, but that eliminating deprivation would be an important part. Anita came back, "Some groups work together, they say, to replant the roots that sustain life." I asked how long betterment initiatives have been around. The answer was, longer than anyone remembered.

Anita complimented heaven's problem solvers: "You may think little committees working on little projects can't be effective. But the need for them grows as we channel."

Then: "I've met scientists trying to develop injections that stand up to environment. They call what they're after peace genes. They hope to convince a medical-scientific board, when they're ready, to approve limited testing in humans. If they get results, they'd add the gene to inoculations for measles, chicken pox or flu shots.

"A sub-group wants to find a cure for AIDS and add peace genes to it, introducing AIDS-peace genes wherever the disease is epidemic or endemic. They're forever testing experimental formulations for toxicity and effectiveness. I can't see us messing with genes but we can get into one of these programs and make ourselves useful.

"Gene scientists try to make love and peace serums resistant to tampering, to infuse our natures with love of peace without exposing pioneers to ruthless neighbors lacking the genes. An aboriginal clique holds that the only effective way to start societies on peace genes is to wipe out all existing species – exactly what God won't listen to."

257

"Other ideas range from skull-imbedded stimulators to mind altering drugs to enhance pleasure. No group has a start-to-finish plan. Maybe, by the time you check in, the challenge will be narrowed or solved. That's how it must have been when human genes were first perfected. Genetic codes, no accidents, were printed out very slowly."

She mentioned a problem she had when meeting new groups. "I tell them about us and the first reaction's always, wait for you to come. I tell them we're trying to make your time on Earth worth something. I feel like a colleague even if I'm only a gadfly."

"One panel has over thirty writers, journalists and former publicists planning to promote change when it comes. They write scenarios about the benefits of human betterment. You'd fit there."

I said, "Been there, done that. No more guilds for this lily. Any husband and wife teams?" She thought so.

I wrote, "God isn't waiting for instructions, but do you think He might go for pyrotechnics to scare criminals into reforming?" She signed off without answering. I didn't think it was a bad idea.

Before long Anita told me about two more groups. "One, close to your heart, looks for a rationale for God to renew His interventions. God never went for their proposal to create new believers by making rivers flow backwards on advertised days – or with instigating floods, famines and pestilences – all rejected."

That crew interested me. "They sound good. What about the other group?"

"They have their eyes on missionary approaches, too - hundreds of thousands to be trained here, returned to their planets as adults protected from harm. Every group harbors the hope that God will invoke His power to make its ideas succeed."

I reminded Anita that I was with them in spirit, but there was no way I'd arrive in heaven, carpetbag in hand, and start huckstering solutions. I liked hearing that others are helping and said there had to be a plan He'll buy, but not from used up rookies.

The idea of masses descending on the planets to preach reason resonated with Anita. "A large, protected movement could go anywhere, see anyone. But *you'd* have to have a rein on your temper." Here I'd been thinking of a cushy cloud desk job in heaven. But she was right, human betterment could mean fieldwork anywhere.

Another betterment group excited Anita. "They're ultra thinkers creating new projects to develop. Their output goes to the core group where I work, which evaluates their reports and assembles talent to develop promising ones. Human betterment here is no lonesome road. It's the oldest do-good society in celestial history."

Anita had become a reader, proofreader and file organizer for the core group. "I attend meetings, summarize reports and research old files.

I don't evaluate them. I just cross-index to make sure a new idea doesn't duplicate an old one.

"Before anything is tried, the core committee must agree it has a chance. I have no clue yet to how proposals move from charts to action. I haven't been at this long."

Later: "File research isn't dull work. I'm glad I'm doing it. When I locate copycats, they're told to try something different."

Two nights later, Anita wrote, "God Himself has evolved. He strikes me as what conservatives would call a bleeding heart liberal. His patience is incredible.

"There are two basic schools of thought about human betterment. Let God do it is one; the other says *we* must discover a reform process He will accept and that one day the right way *will* be found. If God hasn't identified a permanent path to human betterment, the laborers in His vineyards can't feel too guilty that their efforts have yet to succeed."

Anita's letters always return to Him. "Humankinds need to rise to higher ethical levels, live by His truth and avoid doing harm. When nations stop lying to and killing each other, God will help them. I don't think that's being naïve."

Sometimes she was so naïve it was scary. Not long after we moved into Stuyvesant Town, I came home from work and found two strange men sitting with her at our drum table in the living room. I must have looked startled. They got up. Anita said pleasantly, "This is my husband."

I looked from one man to the other, puzzled and concerned. They said they were canvassing the building, trying to interest new families in time shares at some lake. Not politely I said we weren't interested. Anita was embarrassed when I suggested they leave. As soon as they were gone, I asked how they got in. "They rang the doorbell and said, 'Hello, Mrs. Ober'. They knew us. I had to be polite."

I walked her to the door, opened it and pointed below the doorbell where our name was. "That's how they knew. How did _you_ know they weren't rapists?"

She learned from that. Years later when a time share cottage deal had me breathing hard, Anita was the one to turn off the faucet.

Anita was uncomfortable with words like godfather, godsend and god-like. "When did god-speed stop meaning God guide you and become have a nice day?"

Anita was irritated with expressions like god damn, godforsaken and godawful that show disrespect for Him. "I want someone more sincere than money-grubbing revivalists to come forward with the real words of God.

"If God descended to Earth as widely reported, there's no proof of it here. With ten, now nine 'earths' to shepherd, He has a full time job here. Creative clerics say He, as defined by them, tells them what to say. Their sermons quote Him. Does that mean He talks to them now or aren't they forever hunting persuasive parables on their own?

"He wants zeal applied to human betterment, not to making the rich richer and erecting soaring sanctuaries to themselves (one reason there are none here). He wants love, peace and enough for all.

"Now that humankinds have the means to destroy themselves, only multi-national dedication to equalizing the human condition can save them. Where do I get that? Mr. Kincaide lent me a book called, 'The Word,' compiled by a Committee on Devotion, approved by God."

"God doesn't confide in me or in pulpit, radio and television evangelists who tell everyone He wants us to support their transparent fund raising sermons."

Sobered by Anita's observations, I asked if Jews are really the chosen people. Her answer was, "Sure they are. So are all other people. He favors colors equally, too. There'll never be a segregated heaven unless bigot militias take heaven by force."

262

The expression 'chosen people' reminded Anita of a bit of family gossip: "We have un-chosen people." She had talked about an aunt and uncle reunited in heaven. She said not to name them. But when the uncle reincarnated, the aunt didn't.

"Couples reincarnate expecting to continue their love in their next lives. When my aunt refused to go, it meant she didn't want to be his wife again. He was un-chosen."

This popped up in a later letter. I asked, "Has there ever been a palace revolt there? Is God the same God He's always been?" Here's what she channeled:

"He is the same God. Satan was contrived as plotting His downfall and his own ascendancy; but a Satan who never existed couldn't lead a palace revolt."

Before the next letter it occurred to me that light bodies might be deployed to protect people doing God's work on the planets. I bounced it off Anita, who said, "I haven't heard of light bodies leaving heaven. An indestructible group of them on each planet, reinvigorating belief in God - I'll ask if that's possible."

The use of unassailable light bodies interested more people than Anita knew. She later reported, "Light bodies fanning out on the planets at strategic times and places to convince people to turn to God have been proposed. But the answer had to be no.

"The light body is designed for heaven, which has no atmosphere or barometric pressure. Exposure to universes' atmospheres would cause choking. They'd have to be rescued. No purveyor of God's true gospel can be effective outside of heaven in a light body." That news dulled my appetite for quick fixes to large problems.

Anita had more. "Human betterment has inspired dozens of cottage industries here. I talk to people working on one project who mention others. Every group would like to see its theories included in one overall plan.

"They work out ways to overcome human failings and to develop convincing evidence that there's a God. One plan would organize huge meetings, telling under roofs, tents and the sky heavenly truths to change the worlds." It struck me there's too much competition now.

Anita talked more about chemists plugging away at made-in-heaven programs to eliminate diseases of the living, to immunize in the womb against the capacity for evil and to fortify brains with autonomic defenses against aging and accidents, using radar like animals have that can warn ahead of time of impending natural disasters.

"When more durable, safer humans exist, each life will outlast the ones before. Divine purpose is thwarted now because the tethers between heaven and the planets stretch too far. Our spiritual umbilical cords fray in spite of God's efforts. Betterment is a growing challenge. Entrenched power goes deeper than soulless corporate heads; it includes the corrupt at every level.

264

Corruption lurks everywhere. One night I rented a car so Anita and I could attend a banquet honoring the late Peter Goldmark, then head of CBS Laboratories. We were fortunate to find a parking place on 105th Street around the corner from the Academy of Medicine on New York's Upper East Side.

The food was forgettable, the speeches long and predictable. When we returned to the car, it wouldn't start. A downhill slope got us coasting down into Lexington Avenue; still the engine didn't start. I hailed a cab. "It's worth ten dollars to get the car pushed to the nearest garage." We settled for twenty. He knew one on 110th Street.

This wasn't the kind of experience Anita relished. She was pale and frightened by the time we got the last push into a garage presided over by a heavyset, laconic black mechanic. Holding the cab, I popped the hood and asked the proprietor if he could give my battery a boost. He looked under the hood and demanded, "What battery is this?" That's when we learned that it had been stolen.

I called the rental company and asked them to pick up the car and us. Their answer was, buy a new battery and drive it back."

The mechanic heard it and took the phone from my hand. "Either you comes and gets your wheels in twenty minutes or I pushes it back to the street where they eats it!" They said they'd be right over. I tipped my benefactor, gave him the keys and we went home in the cab that pushed us all the way to that street-smart Solomon.

Suddenly, action in heaven! Anita wrote, "A council of groups is being assembled to petition God and His inner circle, complaining that every plan put forward for human betterment is turned down. It will ask for clearer guidelines.

It's a reflection of growing restlessness over what's seen as His continued coddling of His 'mistakes.'"

"God laid down a non-violence policy and leaves it to the groups to figure out how to make it work. We're reminded of that whenever a new plan for improvement, punishment or retribution is rejected. Nobody thinks He'll change His mind, but proponents hope for *some* relaxation of the no punishment dictum."

I said, "A *little* wrath on His part would help."

From another letter: "Discouraged do-gooders are calm, logical and reasonable. Nobody I heard of except your Uncle Harry has challenged God, but some quit human betterment and others say the end *requires* them to keep trying. What do you think?"

"I'm too-recently converted to sound off but I won't throw in the towel before I climb into the ring." It didn't matter what I thought. In the end God thanked the petitioners for their patience and urged more study and planning. Nothing changed.

Her mention of do-gooders recalls the night Anita and I attended a parent-teacher meeting at Hunter Elementary School. Wonder of Manhattan wonders, I found a parking spot immediately on Lexington Avenue just north of the school. That's where my good luck ended. As I alighted from the car, my left shoe plopped dead center into a mound of Manhattan dog do that swallowed my foot to the ankle. Rounding the car, Anita took one look and broke up. Her amusement doubled at my frantic hop to a trashcan for discarded newspaper to scrape off the mess. She laughed all the way to school and pointedly sat away from me, giggling whenever those

266

big brown eyes met mine. For days, I cursed the Gotham golem who turned a mastiff loose on Lexington Avenue for my benefit. Anita always laughed easily, especially when the jokes and/or messes were on me.

Our letters continued almost daily. Anita channeled one night, "In all the millennia, God, too, has learned. It took Him eons to become a God of kindness and tolerance. He has tried longer than history to steer humanity down loving paths. When He exports heaven's love to the planets, betterment groups here can look for other jobs." She added, "Until then some group should develop a bullet proof messiah."

Change of subject: "Some day you'll see our expandable home, the libraries, our parents' homes, my favorite public areas, where the groups meet - and enjoy God's spectacular geography, featuring vast self-controlled lawns under parapets of perennially green shade trees, all the same height, where we appreciate everything we have.

"I have a list of fabulous sights to show you; rolling verdant vistas of incredible beauty, the platform overlooking the ten universes - and we'll go together to classrooms and lecture halls where great minds of the universes teach and learn.

"One awesome feature here is that every gathering place stretches as it fills. We have no special seating or standing arrangements. First come all served! Whoever comes fits. Equal opportunity is as common here as it's rare on the planets."

This later; "Anyone can work in Receiving with a little indoctrination. Not everyone is patient enough to stay with long-term human betterment programs In a Receiving crisis, most ex-receivers drop what we're doing and check in to help. Human betterment groups don't operate in crisis mode. They deliberate and move like turtles.

They evaluate and shape suggestions for new experiments, proposals to God and prepare symposiums. They perform and report on lab experiments. Sub-groups make changes, which are resubmitted until final plans, if approved, go forward."

I felt for Hector Chevigny. "I see why Hector lost patience. What's hot now?"

Anita said, "Besides the petition, behavior change programs without end. Proposals take forever to be approved. Before He sees them, many minds mull over them. Even if a plan's agreed on, complications can start more discussion, change and delay."

Replying to my frequent what's-going-on query, Anita's answer usually was, "No progress" or "Fine tuning ideas and projects." Once she said, "Cynics would say we're spinning our wheels, but there are no cynics here."

I wondered, "*Are* your groups wasting their time?"

She countered, "Did you say time? Hope is eternal in the eternal."

That's where Anita's cumulative thoughts on human betterment end.

Some say Jesus is God, that God and Jesus are the same. Some disagree. Many disagree on the divinity of Christ. Anita wrote that, in her classes in heaven, there was general agreement that every ancient religion and some that still exist disagreed sharply on many issues, including the divinity of Christ.

I was vaguely aware of the issue. When I asked her in recent letters to describe the argument, Anita told me, "Research the divinity question yourself," which led me to ask again for a reasonable explanation of God's tolerance for religions that teach hate and foment violence.

Anita, tired of answering it, asked Marc, the aboriginal who helped us in Part Six, to answer me. You'll read his response shortly and may see as I do why Anita and Marc deflected my question – partly because, as Anita has channeled all along, God believes the evils of the planets are planetary problems and no longer intervenes in them.

They both threw the problem back to me, no scholar or orator in the area of religion, just an old reformed atheist. I have my own opinions and know Anita's are similar to mine. I did not expect to be accused of hating anyone. In showing me the error of my ways, Marc, inadvertently, I think, made me realize what I *should* have hated.

What started on the streets of Dorchester has to end here. The recent letters, which you'll read, are not this book's mission – which is to share with you

Anita's life and afterlife in heaven and how channeling changed my life and saved me from despair.

This book is about our commitment to love forever and to show grievers that they can love and be happy, homosexuals that there is salvation for them, women that their fight for equality is being fought in heaven and all of us can reach out to and find our lost loves, can believe in God and heaven if we don't now, with or without clerical help. Anita's letters talk about the afterlife open to all whether we pray or not, believe now or never did.

I can't bury completely what the recent letters got me into because they're part of my dialogue with Anita. It isn't necessary, however, for this book, to dig up historical arguments in all their gory detail. I won't proselytize, attack, deride or commit offense against what any human or group of humans believe, whether I agree with them or not.

Was Christ divine or human? Or was he both? These questions have been argued long and bloodily and are still hotly debated. As Anita invited me to, I invite you to review for yourself both sides of the written history and decide what you believe.

Anita wrote that comparative religion lecturers use sources other than the writings of doctrinaire clergies. She found it significant that each ancient "religion" and most of those recognized today established their credentials by "inspired" interpretations of phenomena that support their doctrines.

Mythological speculation fueled by managed fear gave rise to scores of deadly rationalizations concocted and enforced by successive emperors, kings and clerics vying for immortality. For example, differences of opinion on Christ's divinity.

Movements that called themselves Christian - Gnosticism, Nestorianism, Monophysitis, Monotheletism and more recently Jehovah's Witnesses, among others, saw Christ as both divine and human.

A keystone of Catholicism is the claim that Christ was born of God and a virgin and is therefore divine. The Church upheld itself in its First Ecumenical Council in Nicaea in 325 CE where a Symbol of Faith, "the Creed," was cobbled, defining as heresy disputing the divinity of Christ. Later Councils of Ephesus in 431 and Chalcedon in 451 didn't end the dispute over divinity. Dissenting groups were excommunicated. Schisms continue to this day.

As to virgin birth, the Buddhists are recorded as making the same claim for Buddha, born in 560 BCE, long before Christ. Taoists said the same thing about Lao-Tse and the Zoroastrians that Zoroaster was to a virgin born.

It doesn't stop there. Ancient Islamic notables Hakim ibn Hizam and Ali, son of Fatima, were also chalked up as virgin births, along with an Aztec god named Hultzilopochli. Two more are Hunahu & Xblanque, ancient Mayan twins, a Huron Indian named Deganawidahand credited with forming the Iroquois Nation in New York State - and not least an esteemed present day seer in India named Sathya Sai Baba.

As you may know, still more recent authors and historians have posed the theory that Christ escaped crucifixion, married and had children with Mary Magdalene. If they're right, Catholicism is wrong about Christ's divinity.

I've gotten that off my chest and Anita takes over again. "Here there's no doubt that our one God takes us *all* for glorious respites until an inner voice whispers to our souls that it's time to reincarnate. Definitions of God's alleged approval and disapproval jump-started most religions. But God never conferred power of life and death on any sect, never hinted that any hierarchy, excluding all others, speaks for him."

WWII: Anita and I were headed for Oregon in late 1943, on a train out of Chicago. Several times she restrained me from taking part in a discussion going on in nearby facing seats where a cluster had formed around a priest. His sanctimonious posturing gagged me but Anita's "Down, boy" prevailed.

My worst stifled reaction was to his soliloquy on admission to heaven. The priest, pressed to explain the criteria for acceptance, held that a cannibal who ate people could get into heaven if no word of "the way" had reached him, but that humans exposed to and rejecting the teachings of the Catholic Church would go to hell What I didn't say on the train, I did when I wrote what we heard for two days in an article printed in "Commentary" after we got home.

This question of who goes to heaven and who to hell is explored in Dante's "Divine Comedy," which postulates in fiendishly graphic detail all levels of hell and purgatory that await anyone but the completely faithful to Catholicism.

Back to Anita: "Many 'religious' institutions have preached obedience to unholy doctrines that incite fear, prejudice, hatred and murder. Some still do. Threats of hell have been used for centuries without repairing human behavior. Most of us are either innately decent or scared righteous. The rest don't change. *Societies* need to stop doing and permitting grievous wrongs. God wants civilizations to clean up their act, to till, harvest and share equally the fruits of living."

A day later: "Performers and sham mystics on the planets give up their deceits here. Genuine spiritualists reincarnate early, hoping their gifts inspire greater numbers in their next lives."

She read my mind again. "Limits to God's control of the destinies of planet people trouble you. He *can* terminate everything He created but God knows He discontinued His life-and-death control over the living."

I asked her if "God knows" wasn't blasphemy. She reminded me with a question, "Do you think God, who won't exclude evildoers from heaven, has spies reporting those using His name frivolously?" I took that to mean no.

Another evening: "I picture Him with a flowing beard but that's just my fancy. He's probably clean-shaven, youthful and sincere like your Brother Harold. If the Good Gentleman reveals Himself to me I'll tell you what He looks like."

"Everyone here talks about Him. Probably visions of Him are unique to each of us. God didn't emerge from a bible. He *was*, *long before anything*

274

began to be written about Him. Scriptural descriptions of Him are as fanciful as my bearded image."

"Here we *know* there's one God. As you learned, Shamans trust the spirits of their ancestors, belief reinforced when they meet them here. Call them Spirits, Guides or Uncle Sylvester, everyone in heaven and on the earths is somebody's ancestor and descendant."

Anita reported the next night: "I tried to find Jesus for you by whooshing to him and it didn't work. I never think myself to God. It seems disrespectful to buttonhole Him. I leave that idea to Tevya.

Anita and I saw three versions of "Fiddler on the Roof," starring as Tevya Zero Mostel, Hershel Bernardi as the milkman who talked to God and in London, Topol, featuring Russian soldiers with cockney accents. Benita and I have seen "Fiddler" once.

There's a revival in Manhattan at this writing but its allure for me has been muted by traffic delays and "cipient" old age. Scenes in that play made us cry, no matter who the actors were and how they spoke their lines. It takes moments like that to remind me that I'm Jewish in my soul, though some orthodox Jews have hotly disputed it.

Anita continued, "We here see God, not a stand-by in case of death or retirement. Nobody here gets old, or has strokes or heart attacks. Why should God?"

I jumped in with, "Do you mean Jesus Christ is not the Son of God?"

Anita said, "The Jewish enclave says no. Believers say yes – some even that they've seen Jesus. Though born a Jew, Jesus isn't here among the Jewish people."

She went on, "God is *felt* as a glowing presence. It's impossible not to be inspired by Him to be the best selves we can. And nobody known to us is running for God's job."

More: "Nobody I ask here has any idea where Jesus is. His believers say He's with God. When I ask where that is, the answer is, 'Follow the Light.'"

Anita brought the question to an informal roundtable of Episcopalians. "Such get-togethers are common, gatherings of eight or nine, four or five, twenty at the most. They don't pray. Religious klatches pay respects to God, God and Jesus, Jesus alone, Buddha, Allah, Eternal Spirit, Divine Principal or whatever else He's been named.

"I enjoyed the Episcopalians. There was no bible, no leader – just discussants. Some still quote biblical phrases and sentences to make or counter a point.

"I asked them where Jesus is. They pointed to the light. 'There.'"

And: "I tried a Methodist klatch. They don't worship here, either. Their love of God is real, but there are no words in His praise. He's known to be embarrassed by devotion. He regards His power as self-evident and doesn't encourage roundtables. He's quoted as preferring civility of man to man over a plethora of psalms in His honor."

276

"The Methodists also believe Jesus is with the Light. I suppose it's so."

But later, as Earth approached Christmas, Anita amended her inquiries into Jesus Christ by quoting a lecturer she and her parents saw. The subject was, "Jesus, Jew, Gentile - God?" The speaker was introduced as Professor James, who taught in United States universities generations ago and has taught here ever since.

"He sketched where and how Jesus was born according to disputed and varied historical accounts. He scoffed at the virgin birth but described Jesus as a thoughtful, God- seeking man, at war with the leaders of his people, ob- sessed with his perceived destiny, as a descendant of King David, to save the Jewish tribes.

"Appalled by the leaders' scorn for the welfare of the poor, Jesus courageously organized a splinter group of like thinkers. The poor took heart from his visions. Many converted to Christ. Worried leaders foreign and domestic plotted to stop him."

Professor James* pointed out that there's no hard evidence on the crucifixion and it was Christ's followers who reported his elevation to heaven. He said that, from then to now, there's been no proof that Jesus *was* crucified, *was*

*Note: Anita suggested I look up John Franklin Jamison, who calls himself in heaven Professor James. He was born in Somerville near Boston and had an outstanding career after graduating from Amherst College in1879 as class valedictorian. He received his first doctorate in history at Johns Hopkins University in 1882, gained recognition as an expert in historiography, helped found the American Historical Association and became the first editor of the "American Historical Review." He eventually moved to Washington, DC, where he became Director of the Department of Historical Research at the Carnegie Institution and in 1928 head of the Division of Manuscripts at the Library of Congress. He died in 1937, taking the name Professor James in heaven after one of his students called him, "Professor James, son."

the Son of God or that he rose from death. He said every part of the theory is open to challenge. He thinks Jesus and Mary Magdalene reincarnated since they're not found here."

Later I reminded Anita that she had said that whatever living people call their God, He's the same God and asked if believers in heaven still haggle over whose is real.

"In the first place," she wrote, "nobody haggles. In the second, we go right on calling Him what we did in our lifetimes. If you think it's confusing that all the inhabited planets call Him different names, it's no problem here. They all translate to God."

In another letter, Anita reflected, "If God were vengeful, the first smitten would be profiteers who misrepresent Him. For thousands of years sham interpreters with no idea what God wants for us have made up doctrines and claimed they came from Him."

Later: "God sees every life as part of Himself, to be preserved for learning, improvement and accomplishment. Yet no peopled world has produced a lasting civilization truly serving all needs, where love immortalizes man and woman, man and man and woman and woman. All true love is encouraged here. Homosexuals aren't ostracized for theirs. Homosexual harassment is a malicious invention, like persecuting Blacks, Jews or any minority - to divide, exploit, terrorize, imprison or kill for profit."

Several of Anita's letters touched on a new fad in heaven, strong codes of ethics for planets' professional organizations, a project suggested by some of God's advisors. My Brother Harold who died as he graduated from law school, worked with legal experts to produce the first code. He memorized it and volunteered to be reborn with the text imprinted in his mind – the way Mozart brought his music to Earth.

Harold was always a gentle boy. I loved him best in my family. But like all of us he had his private side. I had told Anita about the time – I was eleven - I found my Brother Harold, not thirteen, hiding near an old barn behind our King Street house in Dorchester, smoking a cigarette. He urged me to take a puff (so I wouldn't tell on him). I coughed, choked and thought he had killed me. But I never squealed and never smoked. Anita gave up smoking when we started going together – except for a cigarette she had on V-E Day, which she contritely confessed to in her next letter to me at sea. Harold never became a smoker in spite of his one transient transgression.

Getting back to Harold volunteering to be reborn, doubts about the security of a code imprinted in one baby-to-be cooled enthusiasm for returning to Earth in present world conditions. But codes for professions were on their way to becoming obsessions.

Anita reported, "After hearing about Harold's code, Bill Ober decided he'd form a medical group to update the Hippocratic Oath, which he calls 'absolutely virtually obsolete.' Bill wants a new oath, to provide every human being with government-paid medical and dental care, not only Medicare and Medicaid but what he calls 'Medident, a plan with teeth in it.'

"Bill says his erstwhile colleagues will cry socialized medicine, but effective, enforceable public assistance to the poor is pitiful. 'Treatment for the needy should be financed by honest taxes,' says your cousin."

More about codes: "Everybody's getting involved, musicians, scientists, accountants, artists and ex-Wall Street types are all interested in raising the ethical thresholds in their former fields (only in heaven). But she had a word of concern the next night. "Already, codes are overlapping each other like the staccato beats of drum rolls. Finishing them will be slow because so many experts are getting on the bandwagon."

Thanksgiving Day Parades past: Dody at seven on my shoulders on Central Park West, busy little fists pounding my head to the beats of marching bands. Later, timid little Amy, threatened by loud music and huge floats looming overhead, wasn't happy until I took her home. Then Timothy and Michael took turns urging Grampaw to edge us closer to the curb. The parades always ended at 124 West 79th Street, for Anita's turkey feast, served to wild applause, whoops and the sudden silence as serious eating began.

Christmas Eve Anita wrote, "I wish we could get furloughs from heaven for times like Christmas and New Year's and materialize at parties, not just hover about unseen."

December 24th eves, we celebrated Abe Rosenblum's birthday. He gave more than he got, doted contentedly, wassailed as much as Lily allowed – and the family, plus a few Rosenblum pensioners laid waste to Lily's luscious larder. Anita grew up loving holidays, enjoyed dressing up, shopping for traditional foods and desserts, cooking and serving her hungry family and me until the onset of well-earned diabetes.

Anita wrote: "Heaven's Christians remember Christmas Day quietly here. We'd exult if God let us, but Xmas isn't God's birthday anyway and we respect His wishes."

The next night Anita added: "Musical instruments are made in heaven. Craftsmen with the skill in life build them here. Some are nightmares in odd shapes, piping and keyboards, but produce beautiful sounds.

"Some musical instruments do what violins, bass fiddles and cellos do without visible strings or bows. Open areas in their graceful boxes resonate to fingering."

Then: "The universes' systems are too vast and reasoned to have fallen by chance into place. They were *created* from blueprints developed over centuries."

That led Anita to wonder if, when I'm with her, we could write a book about creation of the universes, from records like the ones she used to educate me and by interviewing heaven's aboriginals. My reaction was, "Sufficient unto the afterday the writing therein." (Well, I thought it was cute.)

Anita reported asking one man why he still prayed in heaven. "He said, 'Habit.' "That may apply to the rest here. Everything here is available to all, prayer or not, and we don't have to pray to stay in heaven.

"As you do now, we pray to God if a living loved one is seriously ill. If there's suffering, we pray for a quick cure or quick end. Long fatal diseases shouldn't trap dying people and their families in cauldrons of needless lingering pain."

Then this: "You'd think that, by now, there'd be one planet with life-long health, high ethics and good human relationships. There isn't, but Group geneticists here are convinced that chemical solutions are simply a matter of cut and try.

"They believe that, if they tinker with genetic makeup long enough, sooner or later, permanent love will be a reality. Their formulas mean little to me. I'm supposed to locate records when someone wants them, not know what they mean. I'm a ferret when a scientist has a new idea and wants to know if it's been tried before. I've heard polite equivalents of 'Oh, shit' more than once.

"Even if a new idea doesn't duplicate an earlier one, file notes on similar formulas that failed discourage further inquiry. Geneticists can usually see at a glance if an old attempt invalidates a new proposal or if it's different enough to approve testing."

282

For the final pages of this book, I lined up excerpts from Anita's letters that I think summarize it. Then I asked her how *she'd* like it to end. When she answered on October 31, 2005, I put aside the quotations – some appear later - and added (see Afterword below) parts of three recent letters, the troublemakers mentioned earlier. One letter bluntly suggested an overhaul of my suppressed jaundiced outlook on Boston Catholics (who, when I was a boy, thought every Jew personally killed Christ).

I think what led to the letters in question was my asking, "Do you know when God changed from wrathful to benevolent?"

She began, "Until Krakatoa God punished severely breaches in His covenants conveyed to humanity by angels. But people increasingly put their trust in opportunists who injected their ideas and prejudices between their followers and God. Krakatoa, on the Java Sea island of Rakata (1883) was the last deliberate expression of His wrath. The volcanic island's huge explosion cost over 36,000 lives from tsunamis, the disappearance of the volcano and a sizeable chunk of Rakata island, floods in Sumatra, Jakarta and throughout the region with ripples felt in France, England, Japan and Australia.

"The explosion was rationalized as an act of nature, not of God. That eventually led Him to disavow punitive intervention, to become a God of love alone, concentrating since on harvesting and loving the souls of the dead, purifying and readying them for new lives. Living people today need to find their own way to the truth and will until His experts invent a human chemistry that conditions humanity to recognize the truth."

I asked: "Do Seventh Day Adventists, Scientologists, Mormons, Moonies, Flower Children or any radical group know God better than Jews, Gentiles and Muslims do?"

Anita wrote, "Thousands of religions came and went since humans peopled the planets. Today, some conviction-driven intellectuals insist there's no God at all." Paul von Ward's book, 'God, Genes and Consciousness,' promote AB's, Advanced Beings, as the first teachers. "He's so sure God doesn't exist that he researched every 'maybe' and 'perhaps' in history and legend to 'prove' AB's (capitalized by him), not God (lower case in his text) taught early humans to survive.

"Von Ward may be convinced, but angels, not abs, educated the earliest humans. God, not abs, created the universes, the living, everything needed for survival AND His crown jewels - the human mind and body. It's irrational not to ask - if God didn't create life, what *credible* force did?

"Early humans found their way from fearful worship of *things* to the conclusion that one God created life in all its forms. One God built paradise to receive, restore and recycle spent souls. Evolution that erodes creation like slow-acting acid didn't produce life! Self anointed leaders and sects by the thousands

284

didn't – only God conceived and brought about the cycles of living, dying and living going on ever since."

Before we turn to the second and third of the three letters that re-shaped the end of this book, here **are** some observations by Anita I'd be remiss leaving out:

> "God labored centuries longer than six days to create the peopled worlds and has labored since to improve them. If planets become paradises, heaven will still retrieve and prepare spent souls for their next lives and their next."

> "The concept of incredible afterlives as rewards for unquestioning loyalty helps only hierarchies that gull people into terrible sacrifices in life in exchange for afterlife glory of which there is no proof."

> "We need churches, mosques and synagogues preaching His truth, teaching us love, but not giving spin to His words - we need them to speak for God, not for themselves."

> "Love leaps environmental barriers. But finding your beloved through all of space will be harder in future lives when relationships become interplanetary. Only being here for eternity insures that you and I will *always* be together."

> "When everyone believes in God, the living will visit heaven during their lifetimes – and God *will* visit every peopled planet. When all of us live in peace, all planets will enjoy travel by willing their way, as we do here."

"When the worlds embrace God fully, lives will be longer and healthier, enough produced for every living soul. Life will mean opportunity, rewards and love. Maybe then you and I will leave heaven to enjoy new lifetimes together."

In one of her hundreds of WWII letters, Anita reflected on how beautifully the two of us, as husband and wife, had grown together. Here are two sentences from that letter. "Such a compact universe you and I are, so full of love. If we could sow our devotion everywhere, we'd turn the world into a loving sphere!"

If she knew then what she does now, she'd have said worlds instead of world. Though we don't channel daily as we did, our love is strong as ever and I continue to learn. For example, long after I thought this book was done, completely blown away by what she channeled to me January 4th and 5th, 2006, I added these After Words.

Anita gave up on my question about why God allowed religions launched by connivance, violence and murder access to the souls of their followers. She tried it on Marc, whom you met before. His answer took me by surprise.

"Norman, you learned hate from people taught that persecuting Jews expressed their love of Christ. Despite your anti-Semitic experiences, Anita's love helped you overcome. Educational and philosophical exposure at a university might have leavened your grievances. Thoughtful study of religion in history can, even now, make you more than Anita's messenger and free you to embrace fully God's law of universal love."

Marc continued, "You are closer to God than you know. You have experienced and given great love. Developed lately spiritually, you have yet to separate your embedded quarrel with Irish Catholics from Catholicism.

"Christ himself did not preach hatred. It was a strategy introduced after he died - by ambitious disciples who believed that blaming Jews for his questionable death would strengthen the faith of their followers.

"Irish Catholics, themselves victimized brutally, were not the first or last taught to hate, provoking our Lord to wrath until He foreswore punishing wrongdoing. Some religions, though not all, have tempered considerably their former political connivances, excommunication and murder. Follow their lead, for truth's sake and for yourself."

Before I could protest, Marc turned to other questions I'd raised with Anita. "God *gave* intelligent information to the peopled planets. Advanced beings you read about were aboriginal angels, trained here, given human bodies and settled among early humans, to befriend and teach them survival, development and the word of God.

"With no written records, such lessons, interpreted subjectively, became distorted as they passed to succeeding generations. In time, poor judgment and cupidity all but suppressed the teaching of the angels.

"Early religions preached love of gods, then of God, encouraged hatred of rivals and coveted absolute power. God saw that evolution in man and nature would never end the crises of conscience. So angels' teaching ended."

288

Marc finished, "God will create no more universes nor revive life on Enistor or any other planet that destroys itself until humans give up hatred, greed and power hunger. Still, the most effective places for thoughtful people to look for God together continue to be churches, temples and mosques, where love of God and all mankind, stripped of self service and manipulation, will one day redeem humanity."

The next day Anita asked me what I made of Marc's letter. I said I'd read it five times and thought, except for tagging me as a deep down anti-Catholic, it was a rational summary of what she wrote all along.

I added huffily, "I never met an Italian Catholic I didn't like (all but one I fought as a boy in Dorchester, if you remember). The Boston Irish I lived with started our fight. Most of my adult life in New York I had Irish friends and loved more than a few. How does Marc know about me, anyway? Is he psychic?"

Anita answered, "Blame me. He asked questions and it came out."

Chastened, I quickly recited what I learned from the Lindwalls: "I release all hate and forgive my haters. I forgive myself for hating them" - **and right then, not before, I understood what Marc meant!** "Marc meant that the Irish were bigger victims than I was! If he was trying to tell me I'm mad at the wrong people, why didn't he just say it?"

Anita reminded me that nobody in heaven criticizes, that hatred is planet business and that Marc probably intended to say less than he did.

My quarrel all along was with the ones who participated in the deals that impoverished and killed the Irish physically and economically as methodically as Hitler did the Jews with his gas chambers. England repressed its colonies and wealthy Protestant manufacturers held the Irish as virtual serfs to make money, all but a few who fought the system their own way. Catholics as a class in Ireland were always close to starvation and the churches, Protestant and Catholic, weren't there for the poor.

I never read Leon Uris's "Trinity" before. I got my hands on a copy and read it avidly, a powerful historical novel indicting the English, cold hearted Protestant gentry and complicit Catholic clerics who stood by, all but a few and St. Patrick, as a million Irish starved to death in the potato famine and over a million more fled Ireland to survive.

I asked Anita, "How could their churches permit the Irish Catholics to starve? Where is God in that scenario?"

Anita's rejoinder was, "I hear what you're saying, but they were devout people who, like their ancestors, followed their religious leaders blindly. Norman, if you take their faith away from them, what's left for them? Will they be better off without the unity, spiritual and moral uplift of *caring* clerics – there were many – before and during the tragedy of the Irish? I'm not ready to take that away from them unless we're prepared to give them something better. Are we?"

There it was again, Anita's gift for finding positive ground in a negative scene. She continued, "Churchgoers value sociability, help with personal problems, coming together in peace, having places to pray, meditate and learn.

People who weep find solace in religious institutions. We come of age, marry and hope through our churches to expose our children to higher ethics and better choices."

Anita was reminding me not to blacken organized religion with one brushstroke. Dietrich Bonhoeffer comes to mind, the German theologian, described as an atheist who became one of the anti-Nazi pastors who plotted to assassinate Hitler, helped smuggle Jews out of Germany, was caught and hanged in a concentration camp in 1945. He left a valuable legacy of writings, indicating strong attachment to Jesus, great piety and evangelical as well as existential views of the world.

Continuing Anita's position on organized religions: "Even churches covering up scandals can be havens for the poor, lonely, frightened and sick. At their best, they bring hope to followers. At their worst, one can hope their parishioners wake up to what's in their best interests.

"They need to take charge of the business as well as benefits of their houses of worship. Many have control, dismissing leaders unequal to their vows, giving new clerics short-term contracts, shunning lifetime guarantees that lock in the harmful with the holy until what they stand for is known.

"Firm lay leadership must control church purse and policy; act as shareholders, not genuflecting victims of hierarchies claiming divine mandates to rule their minds." That was channeled in June, 2006.

Doc Lindwall's releasing is my best shot at making a full adjustment to Anita's thinking. I can't yet forgive Cardinals' sins but I say from my heart, God bless humanity, including, b'gorra, the Boston Irish. I owe them understanding, sympathy and perhaps a few tears.

In closing, I need to acknowledge where Anita's letters have taken me: For thirteen years she lovingly led me from atheism to God and belief that life begins, ends and begins again. We both fondly hope that what she taught me about His benevolent fatherhood of the universes and their peoples rubs off on you.

There's no higher calling for humanity than humaneness itself. Agree or disagree, I believe we are closest to God when our souls seek Him one-to-one as Deists do. Discovering that Deists, like Quakers and other believers are organized and participate in religion one-to-one with God is as comforting as it was surprising.

I believe God gave no religion a lock on heaven and that paradise exists for all of us whether we believe that or not. Could I say that when Anita died? No. Do I believe it now? Yes. It has taken me most of my eighty-seven years to learn. God and heaven are the greatest miracles of life and afterlife. I look forward to the end of my life with eager anticipation and without doubts. Anita did this for me.

The only investment *you* need make in order to be where I am is to love God and His people. Practicing makes love perfect.

My journey ends with a salute to the words of a great Englishman, and American revolutionist, Thomas Paine, who wrote in 'Age of Reason' – "I believe

293

in one God and no more; and I hope for happiness beyond this life." He added, "I believe the equality of man and I believe that religious duties consist in doing justice, loving mercy and endeavoring to make our fellow creatures happy."

Lovingly, Norman, with eternal thanks to Anita.

###

ABOUT THE AUTHOR

At 87, Norman Ober finished writing this book thirteen years after Anita's letters began. Working with deadlines all his professional life, he was determined in retirement to give it all the time it needed – and that's what he did.

Norman began work at twelve in Boston, delivering Sunday papers by bike, writing for "The Latin School Register" acting in school productions and later directing and acting in stage plays and portraying mostly villains with a group of actors adapting popular plays and books for presentation on WEEI, Boston.

That start encouraged him to move to New York City where his first professional job was puppeteer, actor and writer with a traveling company. After five years of pulling strings and speaking behind a proscenium, he met Anita. It was love at first sight. He gave up marionettes to make a living in Manhattan and stay close to Anita. He had learned to project dialects and voice changes for marionette characters, brought the knack to network radio and hung on until World War II, when he entered the Navy. Returning three years later to the birth throes of television, a new medium where every voice needed a different face. He turned to writing network radio dramas and print fiction and articles.

Norman and Anita were married during the war. His first postwar job was at WCBS Radio writing broadcast promotion, moved up in twenty-five years at CBS Radio to …but it's all in the book.

For more information, please visit www.anitasheaven.com, or contact Blooming Twig Books at 1-866-389-1482 or info@bloomingtwigbooks.com